Student Guide to the PANDOS Project

The Virtual Square Lab

Michael Goldweber

Xavier University

Renzo Davoli

Università di Bologna

μMPS3, μMPS2, μMPS, MPS, μARM, Kaya, JaeOS, and Pandos are products of the Virtual Square Lab.
See `virtualsquare.org/`
The μMPS3 home page is `virtualsquare.org/umps`

ISBN: 978-1-716-31559-6

Contents

List of Figures

Preface

In my junior year as an undergraduate I took a course titled, "Systems Programming." The goal of this course was for each student to write a small, simple multitasking operating system, in S/360 assembler, for an IBM S/360. The students were given use of a machine emulator, Assist-V, for the development process. Assist, was a S/360 assembler programming environment. (Think SPIM for the 70's.) Assist-V was an extension of Assist that supported privileged instructions in addition to various emulated "attached" devices. The highlight of the course was if your operating system ran correctly (or at least without discernible errors), you would be granted the opportunity, in the dead of night, to boot the University's mainframe, an IBM S/370, with your operating system. (Caveat: The University used VM, IBM's virtual machine technology. Hence students didn't actually boot the whole machine with their OS's, but just one VM partition. Nevertheless, booting/running a VM partition and booting/running the whole machine are isomorphic tasks.) No question, booting and running a handful of tasks concurrently on the University's mainframe with my own OS was one of highlights of my undergraduate education!

My experience of writing a complete operating system repeated itself in graduate school. In this case the machine emulator was the Cornell Hypothetical Instruction Processor (CHIP); a made up architecture that was a cross between a PDP-11 and an IBM S/370. The operating system design was a three phase/layer affair called HOCA by its creator. While there was no real machine to test with, the thrill and sense of accomplishment of successfully completing the task, to say nothing of the many lessons learned throughout the experience were no less than the earlier experience.

In the late 1990's Professor Renzo Davoli and one of his graduate students Mauro Morsiani, in the spirit of both Assist-V/370 and CHIP, created MPS, a MIPS 3000 machine emulator that not only authentically emulated the processor (still no floating point), but also faithfully emulated five different device categories. Furthermore, they updated the HOCA project, which they called TINA, for this new architecture. Once again, students could take their operating system, developed and debugged on MPS (which also contained an excellent debugging facility) and run it unchanged on a real machine.

MPS, with its faithful emulation of the MIPS 3000, though, proved to be too complex for a one semester undergraduate project. Hence Renzo and I set out to create μMPS – a pedagogically appropriate machine emulator appropriate for use by undergraduates. In addition, we updated TINA for this new architecture. That new project was called Kaya.

μMPS and Kaya were originally released in 2004. Kaya was later updated and rereleased in its current form in 2009. In 2011 μMPS was updated by Tomislav Jonjic to μMPS2 with a new GUI and multiprocessor support.

Many lessons have been learned over the years since the introduction of μMPS and Kaya. This led to the development of μMPS3. Perhaps more important than the release of a new machine emulator is the redesign of the accompanying student project, now called Pandos.

While Pandos bears a lot of similarity with Kaya, the reassignment of tasks to phases and reconceptualization of the memory management subsystem will hopefully lead to greater student success. Furthermore, by expanding the number of phases and eliminating the dependencies between phases, there are many more possible project configurations.

A raw machine emulator, such as μMPS3, which is fully described in μMPS3 Principles of Operation [9], can support a wide variety of undergraduate, and graduate-level projects. The Pandos project is just one such project. The Virtual Square Lab, which produced both Pandos and μMPS3 is also currently producing additional projects for μMPS3 as well as for VDE, the Virtual Distributed Ethernet tool also produced by the Virtual Square Lab.

These other projects, like Kaya, are all designed to be accomplished by advanced undergraduates working either solo or in teams in the context of a semester-long multi-phase project.

Renzo and I wish to offer our heartfelt thanks and gratitude to:

- Mauro Morsiani. Mauro generously donated his time to modify MPS into μMPS. μMPS and the accompanying Kaya Project Guide were originally released in 2004.

- Tomislav Jonjic, who updated the GUI and added multiprocessor support, creating μMPS2. μMPS2 is 100% backward compatible with μMPS.

- Marco Melletti, who in 2017, created μARM.

- Mattia Biondi, who graciously and competently undertook the development work in updating μMPS2 to μMPS3.

As the date below indicates, the μMPS3/Pandos project took place during the 2020 Covid-19 pandemic. While my wife and I planned on residing in Bologna, Italy for six months, we returned home to Cincinnati, OH after two and a half months, in March of 2020. Though our time in Bologna was cut short, I wish to thank the University of Bologna in general and Renzo Davoli, my long-time friend and partner in "CS" crime in particular for their hospitality and support.

Finally we wish to thank our wives, Alessandra and Mindy without whose inexhaustible patience projects such as this would never see the light of day.

Michael Goldweber
December, 2020

The least of learning is done in the classrooms.

Thomas Merton

Introduction

The Pandos operating system described below was originally inspired by the T.H.E. system outlined by Dijkstra back in 1968 [4]. Dijkstra's paper described an OS divided into six layers. Each layer i was an ADT or abstract machine to layer $i + 1$; successively building up the capabilities of the system for each new layer to build upon. The operating system described here also contains multiple layers, though Pandos is not as complete as Dijkstra's.

A key design goal of Pandos is to be representatively complete. By this we mean that many of the standard parts of an operating system are present, though in a rather unsophisticated form. For example:

- The scheduler is the simple round-robin algorithm.

- There is a deadlock detector; though very rudimentary.

- There is support for both character-based I/O devices and DMA-based I/O devices, but only two of each type, and only up to eight for each device class.

- The page replacement algorithm is first-in, first-out.

- There is only one exemplar daemon process; the delay daemon.

1

- Inter-process communication is limited to a 32 page shared data space.

- Page Table structures are simple arrays.

- The described implementation of virtual memory provides for multiple optimizations to migrate from a very basic approach (e.g. using **TLBCLR** to resolve TLB cache inconsistencies), to a more sophisticated dedicated disk-based approach for providing a backing store service.

The goal is to learn by doing, particularly with respect to managing complexity. The complexity comes from the subtle interactions between all the moving parts, rather than from the complexity of any single component.

Pandos is actually the latest instantiation of an older "learning" operating system design. Ozalp Babaoglu and Fred Schneider originally described a pedagogical operating system, calling it the HOCA OS [3], for implementation on the Cornell Hypothetical Instruction Processor (CHIP) [1, 2]. Later, Renzo Davoli and Mauro Morsiani reworked HOCA, calling it TINA [11] and ICAROS [10], for implementation on the Microprocessor (without) Pipeline Stages (MPS) [11, 12]. A couple of years after TINA saw the development of Kaya [6] for implementation on μMPS [5] and later, μMPS2 [8, 7].

Pandos is the latest revamping-modernization of this design for implementation on μMPS3 [9].

Level 0: The base hardware of μMPS3.
Though μMPS3 carries the designation of "3," it is NOT backward compatible for operating system code developed for μMPS or μMPS2.

Level 1: The additional services provided in BIOS. This includes the services provided by the BIOS-Excpt handler, the BIOS-TLB-Refill handler, and the additional BIOS services/instructions (i.e. **LDST**, **LDCXT**, **PANIC**, and **HALT**).

The μMPS3 Principles of Operation [9] contains a complete description of both Level 0 and 1.

Level 2: The Queues Manager (Phase 1 – described in Chapter 2). Based on the key operating systems concept that active entities at one layer are just data structures at lower layers, this layer supports the management of queues of structures: *pcb*'s.

Level 3: The Kernel (Phase 2 – described in Chapter 3). This level implements eight new kernel-mode process management and synchronization primitives in addition to multiprogramming, a process scheduler, device interrupt handlers, and deadlock detection.

Level 4: The Support Level - The Basics (Phase 3 – described in Chapter 4). Level 3 is extended to support a system that can support multiple user-level processes that each run in their own virtual address space. Furthermore, support is provided to read/write to character-oriented devices.

Level 5: DMA Device Support (Phase 4 – described in Chapter 5). An extension of Level 4 providing I/O support for DMA devices: disk drives and flash devices. Furthermore, this level optionally implements a more realistic backing store implementation.

Level 6: The Delay Facility (Phase 5 – described in Chapter 6). This level provides the Support Level with a sleep/delay facility.

Level 7: Cooperating User Processes (Phase 6 – described in Chapter 7). This level introduces a shared memory space and user-level synchronization primitives to facilitate cooperating processes.

Optionally, one can continue developing Pandos with

Level 8: The File System (Phase 7) This level implements the abstraction of a flat file system by implementing primitives necessary to create, rename, delete, open, close, and modify files.

Level 9: Networking support (Phase 8)

Level 10: The Interactive Shell (Phase 9) – why not?

1.1 Project Configuration

The basic one semester senior-level undergraduate project consists of Phases 1-3. This project can be undertaken by individual students or small student teams (e.g. pairs). For those concerned with time constraints, Phase 1, which is essentially a data structures assignment, can be skipped. Instead, students would work with instructor provided Phase 1 code. These three phases are cumulative, however, and cannot be skipped.

Phases 4-9, the Advanced Layers, are not cumulative. One can pick and choose which phases to implement and in which order. While there are no hard dependencies between these phases, there are some soft logical ones. (e.g. An interactive shell before a file system, while possible, is of limited use.) Finally, only phases 4-6 are given a detailed treatment in this guide.

1.2   Directory Structure

Since one develops Pandos in phases, the following directory structure is recommended:

```
/pandos
  /h
  /phase1
  /phase2
  /phase3
    ...
  /testers
```

1.3   Notational conventions

- Words being defined are *italicized*.

- Register, fields and instructions are **bold**-marked.

- Field **F** of register **R** is denoted **R.F**.

- Bits of storage are numbered right-to-left, starting with 0.

- The i-th bit of a storage unit named **N** is denoted **N**[i].

- Memory addresses and operation codes are given in hexadecimal and displayed in big-endian format.

- All diagrams illustrate memory and going from low addresses to high addresses using a left to right, bottom to top orientation.

- Cross references to other Sections or Chapters where one can find more detailed information are enclosed in square brackets: [Section 1.3]

- References to the μMPS3 Principles of Operation [9] will have a *pops* suffix. e.g. A reference to the chapter on Exception Handling will be denoted: [Chapter 3-*pops*]

1.4   File Locations

In the Unix world there is a fundamental difference between packages installed from source and those installed via a package manager with regard to the installation location of supporting files (include files, libraries, etc). [Appendix H-*pops*]

All file locations described in this guide assume installation via a package manager. See Appendix H in the μMPS3 Principles of Operation [9] for how to adjust these locations when working on an installation created from source files.

Part I
The Pandos Core

UNIX is basically a simple operating system, but you have to be a genius to understand the simplicity.

Dennis Ritchie

Phase 1 - Level 2: The Queues Manager

Level 2 of Pandos instantiates the key operating system concept that active entities at one layer are just data structures at lower layers. In this case, the active entities at a higher level are processes (i.e. programs in execution) and the data structure(s) that represent them at this level are *process control blocks* (*pcb*s).

7

```
/* process control block type */
typedef struct pcb_t {
    /* process queue fields */
    struct pcb_t        *p_next,        /* pointer to next entry */
                        *p_prev,        /* pointer to prev entry */

    /* process tree fields */
                        *p_prnt,        /* pointer to parent      */
                        *p_child,       /* pointer to 1st child   */
                        *p_sib;         /* pointer to sibling      */

    /* process status information */
    state_t             p_s;            /* processor state */
    cpu_t               p_time;         /* cpu time used by proc */
    int                 *p_semAdd;      /* pointer to sema4 on    */
                                        /* which process blocked */

    /* support layer information */
    support_t           *p_supportStruct;
                                        /* ptr to support struct */
} pcb_t;
```

The queue manager will implement four *pcb* related sets of functions:

- The allocation and deallocation of *pcb*s.

- The maintenance of queues of *pcb*s.

- The maintenance of trees of *pcb*s.

- The maintenance of a single sorted list of *active semaphore descriptors*, each of which supports a queue of *pcb*s: The ASL.

2.1   The Allocation and Deallocation of *pcb*s

One may assume that Pandos supports no more that *MAXPROC* concurrent processes; where MAXPROC should be set to 20 (in the const.h) file.[1] Thus this level needs a "pool" of MAXPROC *pcb*s to allocate from and deallocate to. Assuming that there is a set of MAXPROC *pcb*s, the free or unused ones can be kept on a NULL-terminated single, linearly linked list (using the p_next field), called the *pcbFree* List, whose head is pointed to by the variable pcbFree_h.

To support the allocation and deallocation of *pcb*s there should be the following three externally visible functions:

- *pcb*s which are no longer in use can be returned to the pcbFree list by using the method:
  ```
  void freePcb(pcb_t *p)
  ```

    /* Insert the element pointed to by p onto the pcbFree list. */

- *pcb*s should be allocated by using:
  ```
  pcb_t *allocPcb()
  ```

    /* Return NULL if the pcbFree list is empty. Otherwise, remove
    an element from the pcbFree list, provide initial values for ALL
    of the *pcb*s fields (i.e. NULL and/or 0) and then return a pointer
    to the removed element. *pcb*s get reused, so it is important that
    no previous value persist in a *pcb* when it gets reallocated. */

There is still the question of how one acquires storage for MAXPROC *pcb*s and gets these MAXPROC *pcb*s initially onto the pcbFree list. Unfortunately, there is no malloc() feature to acquire dynamic (i.e. non-automatic) storage that will persist for the lifetime of the OS and not just the lifetime of the function they are declared in. Instead, the storage for the MAXPROC *pcb*s will be allocated as *static* storage. A static array of MAXPROC *pcb*s will be declared in initPcbs(). Furthermore, this method will insert each of the MAXPROC *pcb*s onto the pcbFree list.

- To initialize the pcbFree List:
  ```
  initPcbs()
  ```

---

[1]A supplied "starter" version of const.h can be found in/usr/include/umps3/umps

/* Initialize the pcbFree list to contain all the elements of the static array of MAXPROC *pcb*s. This method will be called only once during data structure initialization. */

2.2   Process Queue Maintenance

The methods below do not manipulate a particular queue or set of queues. Instead they are generic queue manipulation methods; one of the parameters is a pointer to the queue upon which the indicated operation is to be performed.

The queues of *pcb*s to be manipulated, which are called *process queues*, are all double, circularly linked lists, via the p_next and p_prev pointer fields. Instead of a head pointer, each queue will be pointed at by a tail pointer.

To support process queues there should be the following externally visible functions:

```
pcb_t *mkEmptyProcQ()
```

/* This method is used to initialize a variable to be tail pointer to a process queue.
Return a pointer to the tail of an empty process queue; i.e. NULL. */

```
int emptyProcQ(pcb_t *tp)
```

/* Return TRUE if the queue whose tail is pointed to by tp is empty. Return FALSE otherwise. */

```
insertProcQ(pcb_t **tp, pcb_t *p)
```

/* Insert the *pcb* pointed to by p into the process queue whose tail-pointer is pointed to by tp. Note the double indirection through tp to allow for the possible updating of the tail pointer as well. */

```
pcb_t *removeProcQ(pcb_t **tp)
```

/* Remove the first (i.e. head) element from the process queue whose tail-pointer is pointed to by tp. Return NULL if the process queue was initially empty; otherwise return the pointer to the removed element. Update the process queue's tail pointer if necessary. */

```
pcb_t *outProcQ(pcb_t **tp, pcb_t *p)
```

/* Remove the *pcb* pointed to by p from the process queue whose tail-pointer is pointed to by tp. Update the process queue's tail pointer if necessary. If the desired entry is not in the indicated queue (an error condition), return NULL; otherwise, return p. Note that p can point to any element of the process queue. */

```
pcb_t *headProcQ(pcb_t *tp)
```

/* Return a pointer to the first *pcb* from the process queue whose tail is pointed to by tp. Do not remove this *pcb* from the process queue. Return NULL if the process queue is empty. */

2.3   Process Tree Maintenance

In addition to possibly participating in a process queue, *pcb*s are also organized into trees of *pcb*s, called *process trees*. The p_prnt, p_child, and p_sib pointers are used for this purpose.

The process trees should be implemented as follows. A parent *pcb* contains a pointer (p_child) to a NULL-terminated single, linearly linked list of its child *pcb*s. Each child process has a pointer to its parent *pcb* (p_prnt) and possibly the next child *pcb* of its parent (p_sib). For greater efficiency you may want to make the linked list of child *pcb*s a NULL-terminated double, linearly linked list.

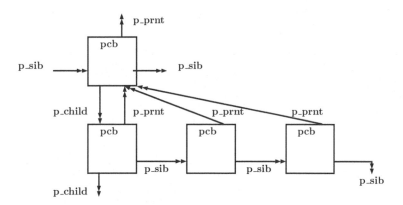

Figure 2.1: Process Tree

To support process trees there should be the following externally visible functions:

```
int emptyChild(pcb_t *p)
```

/* Return TRUE if the *pcb* pointed to by p has no children. Return FALSE otherwise. */

`insertChild(pcb_t *prnt, pcb_t *p)`

/* Make the *pcb* pointed to by p a child of the *pcb* pointed to by `prnt`. */

`pcb_t *removeChild(pcb_t *p)`

/* Make the first child of the *pcb* pointed to by p no longer a child of p. Return NULL if initially there were no children of p. Otherwise, return a pointer to this removed first child *pcb*. */

`pcb_t *outChild(pcb_t *p)`

/* Make the *pcb* pointed to by p no longer the child of its parent. If the *pcb* pointed to by p has no parent, return NULL; otherwise, return p. Note that the element pointed to by p need not be the first child of its parent. */

2.4   The Active Semaphore List (ASL)

A *semaphore* is an important operating system concept. While understanding semaphores is not yet needed, this level nevertheless implements an important data structure/abstraction which supports Pandos's implementation of semaphores.

For the purpose of this level it is sufficient to think of a semaphore as an integer. Associated with this integer is:

- An address; semaphores, like all integers, have a physical address in memory.

- A process queue.

A semaphore is *active* if there is at least one *pcb* on the process queue associated with it. (i.e. The process queue is not empty: `emptyProcQ(s_procq)` is FALSE.)

The following implementation is suggested: Maintain a sorted NULL-terminated single, linearly linked list (using the `s_next` field) of semaphore descriptors whose head is pointed to by the variable `semd_h`. The list `semd_h` points to will represent the *Active Semaphore List* (ASL). Keep the ASL sorted in ascending order using the s_semAdd field as the sort key.

```
/* semaphore descriptor type */
typedef struct semd_t {
    struct semd_t  *s_next;     /* next element on the ASL */
    int            *s_semAdd;   /* pointer to the semaphore*/
    pcb_t          *s_procQ;    /* tail pointer to a       */
                                /* process queue           */
} semd _t;
```

Maintain a second list of semaphore descriptors, the *semdFree* list, to hold the unused semaphore descriptors. This list, whose head is pointed to by the variable semdFree_h, is kept, like the pcbFree list, as a NULL-terminated single, linearly linked list (using the s_next field).

The semaphore descriptors themselves should be declared, like the *pcb*s, as a static array of size MAXPROC of type semd_t.

There is no reason to make the ASL doubly linked.

For greater ASL traversal efficiency it is STRONGLY recommended to place a dummy node at both the head (s_semAdd ← 0) and tail (s_semAdd ← MAXINT) of the ASL; in which case the size of the static array will increase by two. This is an important programming technique that illustrates the time vs space trade off in programming; sacrifice a small amount of space for a significant speed up in code speed. In this case, the ASL traversal code will no longer need conditionals checking boundary conditions at either end.

To support the ASL there should be the following externally visible functions:

```
int insertBlocked(int *semAdd, pcb_t *p)
```

> /* Insert the *pcb* pointed to by p at the tail of the process queue associated with the semaphore whose physical address is semAdd and set the semaphore address of p to semAdd. If the semaphore is currently not active (i.e. there is no descriptor for it in the ASL), allocate a new descriptor from the semdFree list, insert it in the ASL (at the appropriate position), initialize all of the fields (i.e. set s_semAdd to semAdd, and s_procq to mkEmptyProcQ()), and proceed as above. If a new semaphore descriptor needs to be allocated and the semdFree list is empty, return TRUE. In all other cases return FALSE.
> */

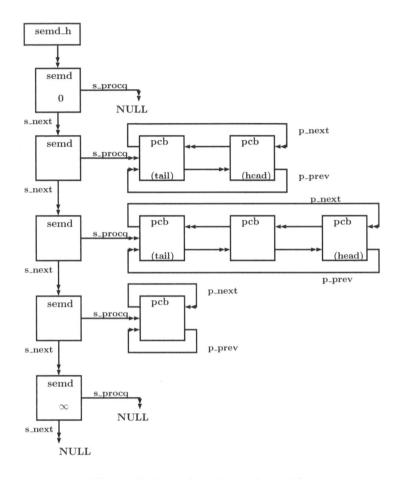

Figure 2.2: Active Semaphore List

```
pcb_t *removeBlocked(int *semAdd)
```

/* Search the ASL for a descriptor of this semaphore. If none is found, return NULL; otherwise, remove the first (i.e. head) *pcb* from the process queue of the found semaphore descriptor and return a pointer to it. If the process queue for this semaphore becomes empty (`emptyProcQ(s_procq)` is TRUE), remove the semaphore descriptor from the ASL and return it to the semdFree list. */

```
pcb_t *outBlocked(pcb_t *p)
```

/* Remove the *pcb* pointed to by p from the process queue associated with p's semaphore (p→ `p_semAdd`) on the ASL. If *pcb* pointed to by p does not appear in the process queue associated with p's semaphore, which is an error condition, return NULL; otherwise, return p. */

```
pcb_t *headBlocked(int *semAdd)
```

/* Return a pointer to the *pcb* that is at the head of the process queue associated with the semaphore `semAdd`. Return NULL if `semAdd` is not found on the ASL or if the process queue associated with `semAdd` is empty. */

```
initASL(
```

/* Initialize the semdFree list to contain all the elements of the array
static `semd_t semdTable[MAXPROC]`
This method will be only called once during data structure initialization. */

Technical Point: Strive to structure the ASL code so that there is one internal/helper function that traverses the ASL and is used by `insertBlocked`, `removeBlocked`, `outBlocked`, and `headBlocked`.

2.5 Nuts and Bolts

There is no one right way to implement the functionality of this level. The recommended approach is to create two modules (i.e. files): one for the ASL and one for *pcb* initialization/allocation/deallocation, process queue maintenance, and process tree maintenance.

The second module, pcb.c, in addition to the public and HIDDEN/private helper functions, will also contain the declaration for the private global variable that points to the head of the pcbFree list.

```
HIDDEN pcb_t *pcbFree_h;
```

The ASL module, asl.c, in addition to the public and HIDDEN/private helper functions, will also contain the declarations for semd_h and semdFree_h

```
HIDDEN semd_t *semd_h, *semdFree_h;
```

Since the ASL module will make calls to the process queue module to manipulate the process queue associated with each active semaphore, this module should

```
#include "pcb.h"
```

This will insure that the ASL can only use the externally visible functions from pcb.c for maintaining its process queues.

Furthermore, the declaration for `pcb_t` would then be placed in the types.h file.[2] This is because many other modules will need to access this definition. The declaration for `semd_t` can be placed in either asl.c (because no other module will ever need to access this definition), or types.h.

2.6 Testing

There is a provided test file, p1test.c that will "exercise" your code. [Appendix A]

As with any non-trivial system, you are strongly encouraged to use the *make* program to maintain your code. A sample *Makefile* has been supplied for you to use. See Chapter 10 in the POPS reference for more compilation details.

Once your (three?) source files have been correctly compiled, linked together (with appropriate linker script, `crtso.o`, and `libumps.o`), and post-processed with umps3-elf2umps (all performed by the sample *Makefile*), your code can be tested by launching the μMPS3 emulator. At a terminal prompt, enter:

umps3

The test program reports on its progress by writing messages to TERMINAL0. These messages are also added to one of two memory buffers; `errbuf` for error messages and `okbuf` for all other messages. At the conclusion of the test program, either successful or unsuccessful, μMPS3 will display a final message and then enter an infinite loop. The final message will either be System Halted for successful termination, or Kernel Panic for unsuccessful termination.

---

[2]A supplied "starter" version of types.h can be found in /usr/include/umps3/umps

The best way to prepare [to be a programmer] is to write programs, and to study great programs that other people have written. In my case, I went to the garbage cans at the Computer Science Center and fished out listings of their operating system.

Bill Gates

3

Phase 2 - Level 3: The Nucleus

Level 3, the Nucleus, builds on the previous levels in two key ways:

1. Receives control from the exception handling facility of Level 1. There are two categories of exceptions [Chapter 3-*pops*]:

   - TLB-Refill events, a relatively frequent occurrence which is triggered during address translation when no matching entries are found in the TLB. Since address translation will not be introduced until the Support Level, the handling of TLB-Refill events is delayed until then.

   - All other exception types, including device/timer interrupts, which, by definition, occur infrequently. This category can be further broken down into
     - Interrupts: peripheral devices and internal timers
     - System Service calls (**SYSCALL**)
     - TLB exceptions - exceptions related to the memory management unit (MMU)
     - Program Trap exceptions (e.g. Bus Error)

2. Using the data structures from Level 2 [Chapter 2], and the facility to handle both system service calls and device interrupts, timer interrupts in particular, provide a process scheduler – support multiprogramming.

Hence, the purpose of the Nucleus is to provide an environment in which asynchronous sequential processes (i.e. heavyweight threads) exist, each making forward progress as they take turns sharing the processor. Furthermore, the Nucleus provides these processes with exception handling routines, low-level synchronization primitives, and a facility for "passing up" the handling of Program Trap, TLB exceptions and certain **SYSCALL** requests to the Support Level. [Chapter 4]

<u>**Important Point:**</u> Since virtual memory is not supported until the Support Level, all addresses at this level are assumed to be physical addresses.

In summary, after some one-time Nucleus initialization code, the Nucleus will repeatedly dispatch a process, i.e. remove a *pcb* from the Ready Queue and perform a **LDST** on the processor state stored in the *pcb* (p_s). This *Current Process* will run until:

- It makes a system call (**SYSCALL**). The Nucleus will handle the system call or pass along the handling to the Support Level. Some system calls block the Current Process - the *pcb* is placed on the ASL and the Scheduler is called to dispatch the next job. If the system call is non-blocking, control is returned to the Current Process.

- It terminates; which is signaled via a system call. The Nucleus will call the Scheduler to dispatch the next process on the Ready Queue.

- The timer assigned to the Scheduler generates an interrupt; the Current Process's quantum/time slice has expired. Its *pcb* is enqueued back on the Ready Queue and the Scheduler is called to dispatch the next job.

- A device interrupt occurs (exclusive of the timer assigned to the Scheduler). The interrupt is acknowledged, and the device's status code is passed along to the *pcb* (i.e. process) that got unblocked as a result of the interrupt; the *pcb* that was waiting for the I/O to complete. The newly unblocked *pcb* is enqueued back on the Ready Queue and control is returned to the Current Process.

- If the Scheduler ever discovers that the Ready Queue is empty it will either **HALT** execution (no more processes to run), **WAIT** for an I/O to complete (which will unblock a *pcb* and populate the Ready Queue), or **PANIC** (halt execution in the presence of deadlock).

Hence the Nucleus's functionality can be broken down into five main categories:

- Nucleus initialization. [Section 3.1]

- The Scheduler. [Section 3.2]

- **SYSCALL** processing. [Section 3.5]

- Device interrupt handler. [Section 3.6]

- The passing up of the handling of all other events. This includes TLB-Refill events [Section 3.3], **SYSCALL**s not handled at this level, page faults, Program Trap exceptions, etc. [Section 3.7]

3.1 Nucleus Initialization

Every program needs an entry point (i.e. `main()`). The entry point for Pandos performs the Nucleus initialization, which includes:

1. Declare the Level 3 global variables. This should include:

   - Process Count: integer indicating the number of started, but not yet terminated processes.

   - Soft-block Count: A process can be either in the "ready," "running," or "blocked" (also known as "waiting") state. This integer is the number of started, but not terminated processes that in are the "blocked" state due to an I/O or timer request.

   - Ready Queue: Tail pointer to a queue of *pcb*s that are in the "ready" state.

   - Current Process: Pointer to the *pcb* that is in the "running" state, i.e. the current executing process.

   - Device Semaphores: The Nucleus maintains one integer semaphore for each external (sub)device in μMPS3, plus one additional semaphore to support the Pseudo-clock. [Section 3.6.3]
     Since terminal devices are actually two independent sub-devices, the Nucleus maintains two semaphores for each terminal device. [Section 5.7-*pops*]

2. Populate the Processor 0 Pass Up Vector. The Pass Up Vector is part of the BIOS Data Page, and for Processor 0, is located at 0x0FFF.F900. [Section 8.5-*pops*]

   The Pass Up Vector is where the BIOS finds the address of the Nucleus functions to pass control to for both TLB-Refill events and all other exceptions. Specifically,

   - Set the Nucleus TLB-Refill event handler address to

     ```
     xxx->tlb_refll_handler =
                 (memaddr) uTLB_RefillHandler;
     ```

     where `memaddr`, in **types.h**, has been aliased to `unsigned int`. Since address translation is not implemented until the Support Level, `uTLB_RefillHandler` is a place holder function whose code is provided. [Section 3.3] This code will then be replaced when the Support Level is implemented.

   - Set the Stack Pointer for the Nucleus TLB-Refill event handler to the top of the Nucleus stack page: 0x2000.1000. Stacks in μMPS3 grow down.

   - Set the Nucleus exception handler address to the address of your Level 3 Nucleus function (e.g. `foobar`) that is to be the entry point for exception (and interrupt) handling [Section 3.4]:

     ```
     xxx->exception_handler = (memaddr) fooBar;
     ```

   - Set the Stack pointer for the Nucleus exception handler to the top of the Nucleus stack page: 0x2000.1000.

3. Initialize the Level 2 (phase 1 - see Chapter 2) data structures:
   ```
   initPcbs()
   initSemd()
   ```

4. Initialize all Nucleus maintained variables: Process Count (0), Soft-block Count (0), Ready Queue (`mkEmptyProcQ()`), and Current Process (NULL). Since the device semaphores will be used for synchronization, as opposed to mutual exclusion, they should all be initialized to zero.

5. Load the system-wide Interval Timer with 100 milliseconds. [Section 3.6.3]

6. Instantiate a single process, place its *pcb* in the Ready Queue, and increment Process Count. A process is instantiated by allocating a *pcb* (i.e. `allocPcb()`), and initializing the processor state that is part of the *pcb*. In particular this process needs to have interrupts enabled, the processor Local Timer enabled, kernel-mode on, the **SP** set to RAMTOP (i.e. use the last RAM frame for its stack), and its **PC** set to the address of `test`. Furthermore, set the remaining *pcb* fields as follows:

   - Set all the Process Tree fields to NULL.

   - Set the accumulated time field (`p_time`) to zero.

   - Set the blocking semaphore address (`p_semAdd`) to NULL.

   - Set the Support Structure pointer (`p_supportStruct`) to NULL.

   Important Point: When setting up a new processor state one must set the *previous* bits (i.e. **IEp & KUp**) and not the *current* bits (i.e. **IEc & KUc**) in the **Status** register for the desired assignment to take effect after the initial **LDST** loads the processor state. [Section 7.4-*pops*]

   Test is a supplied function/process that will help you debug your Nucleus. One can assign a variable (i.e. the **PC**) the address of a function by using

   ```
   yyy->p_s.s_pc = (memaddr) test;
   ```

   Remember to declare *test* as "external" in your program by including the line:

   ```
   extern void test();
   ```

   For rather technical reasons, whenever one assigns a value to the **PC** one must also assign the same value to the general purpose register **t9**. (a.k.a. `s_t9` as defined in **types.h**.) [Section 10.2-*pops*]

7. Call the Scheduler.

Once `main()` calls the Scheduler its task is complete since control should never return to `main()`. At this point the only mechanism for re-entering the Nucleus is through an exception; which includes device interrupts. As long as there are processes to run, the processor is executing instructions on their behalf and only temporarily enters the Nucleus long enough to handle a device interrupt or exception when they occur.

At boot/reset time the Nucleus is loaded into RAM beginning with the second frame of RAM: 0x2000.1000. The first frame of RAM is reserved for the Nucleus stack. Furthermore, Processor 0 will be in kernel-mode with all interrupts masked, and the processor Local Timer disabled. The **PC** is assigned 0x2000.1000 and the **SP**, which was initially set to 0x2000.1000 at boot-time, will now be some value less, due to the activation record for `main()` that now sits on the stack. [Section 8.2-*pops*]

3.2   The Scheduler

Your Nucleus should guarantee finite progress; consequently, every ready process will have an opportunity to execute. The Nucleus should implement a simple preemptive round-robin scheduling algorithm with a time slice value of 5 milliseconds.

Preemptive cpu scheduling requires the use of an interrupt generating system clock. μMPS3 offers two choices: the single system-wide Interval Timer or a processor's Local Timer (PLT). [Section 4.1-*pops*]

One should use the PLT to support per processor scheduling since the Interval Timer is reserved for implementing Pseudo-clock ticks. [Section 3.6.3]

In its simplest form whenever the Scheduler is called it should dispatch the "next" process in the Ready Queue.

1. Remove the *pcb* from the head of the Ready Queue and store the pointer to the *pcb* in the Current Process field.

2. Load 5 milliseconds on the PLT. [Section 4.1.4-*pops*]

3. Perform a Load Processor State (**LDST**) on the processor state stored in *pcb* of the Current Process (p_s).

Dispatching a process transitions it from a "ready" process to a "running" process.

The Scheduler should behave in the following manner if the Ready Queue is empty:

1. If the Process Count is zero invoke the **HALT** BIOS service/instruction. [Section 7.3.7-*pops*] Consider this a job well done!

2. If the Process Count > 0 and the Soft-block Count > 0 enter a *Wait State.* A Wait State is where the processor is not executing instructions, but "twiddling its thumbs" waiting for a device interrupt to occur. μMPS3 supports a **WAIT** instruction expressly for this purpose. [Section 7.2.2-*pops*]

   <u>**Important Point:**</u> Before executing the **WAIT** instruction, the Scheduler must first set the **Status** register to enable interrupts **and** either disable the PLT (also through the **Status** register), or load it with a very large value. The first interrupt that occurs after entering a Wait State should not be for the PLT.

3. Deadlock for Pandos is defined as when the Process Count > 0 and the Soft-block Count is zero. Take an appropriate deadlock detected action; invoke the **PANIC** BIOS service/instruction. [Section 7.3.6-*pops*]

3.3   TLB-Refill events

As outlined above [Section 3.1], the Processor 0 Pass Up Vector's Nucleus TLB-Refill event handler address should be set to the address of your TLB-Refill event handler (e.g. uTLB_RefillHandler)

The code for this function, for Level 3/Phase 2 testing purposes should be as follows:

```
void uTLB_RefillHandler () {
    setENTRYHI(0x80000000);
    setENTRYLO(0x00000000);
    TLBWR();
    LDST ((state_PTR) 0x0FFFF000);
}
```

Writers of the Support Level (Level 4/Phase 3) will replace/overwrite the contents of this function with their own code/implementation.

3.4   Exception Handling

As described above [Section 3.1], at startup, the Nucleus will have populated the Processor 0 Pass Up Vector with the address of the Nucleus exception handler (`fooBar`) and the address of the Nucleus stack page (0x2000.1000). Therefore, if the Pass Up Vector was correctly initialized, `fooBar` will be called (with a fresh stack) after each and every exception, exclusive of TLB-Refill events. Furthermore, the processor state at the time of the exception (the *saved exception state*) will have been stored (for Processor 0) at the start of the BIOS Data Page (0x0FFF.F000). [Section 3.2.2-*pops*]

The *cause* of this exception is encoded in the **.ExcCode** field of the **Cause** register (**Cause.ExcCode**) in the saved exception state. [Section 3.3-*pops*]

- For exception code 0 (Interrupts), processing should be passed along to your Nucleus's device interrupt handler. [Section 3.6]

- For exception codes 1-3 (TLB exceptions), processing should be passed along to your Nucleus's TLB exception handler. [Section 3.7.3]

- For exception codes 4-7, 9-12 (Program Traps), processing should be passed along to your Nucleus's Program Trap exception handler. [Section 3.7.2]

- For exception code 8 (**SYSCALL**), processing should be passed along to your Nucleus's **SYSCALL** exception handler. [Section 3.5]

Hence, the entry point for the Nucleus's exception handling is in essence a case statement that performs a multi-way branch depending on the cause of the exception.

Important Point: To determine if the Current Process was executing in kernel-mode or user-mode, one examines the **Status** register in the saved exception state. In particular, examine the *previous* version of the **KU** bit (**KUp**) since the processor's exception handling circuitry will have performed a stack push on the **KU/IE** stacks in the **Status** register before the exception state was saved. [Section 3.1-*pops*]

3.5   SYSCALL Exception Handling

A System Call (**SYSCALL**) exception occurs when the **SYSCALL** assembly instruction is executed.

By convention, the executing process places appropriate values in the general purpose registers **a0** – **a3** immediately prior to executing the **SYSCALL** instruction. The Nucleus will then perform some service on behalf of the process executing the **SYSCALL** instruction depending on the value found in **a0**.

In particular, if the process making a **SYSCALL** request was in kernel-mode and **a0** contained a value in the range [1..8] then the Nucleus should perform one of the services described below.

3.5.1   Create_Process (SYS1)

When requested, this service causes a new process, said to be a *progeny* of the caller, to be created. **a1** should contain a pointer to a processor state (state_t *). This processor state is to be used as the initial state for the newly created process. The process requesting the SYS1 service continues to exist and to execute. If the new process cannot be created due to lack of resources (e.g. no more free *pcb*'s), an error code of -1 is placed/returned in the caller's **v0**, otherwise, return the value 0 in the caller's **v0**.

Good design calls for tight/strong cohesion and loose coupling between modules/classes/OS Levels, etc. Level 2 implements *pcb*s, and Level 3 utilizes queues of *pcb*s to create a basic multiprogramming environment. However, it is the Support Level that handles address translation as well as all exceptions beyond I/O interrupts and the first eight system calls (and then, only if in kernel-mode). The design question then is how to provide Support Level access to *pcb* fields that will only be used in the Support Level.

The standard approach, at least in systems-level programming such as an OS, is to define a structure containing the additional Support Level fields (support_t) and then add a pointer (support_t *) to the *pcb*. The Support Level code needing access to these fields will execute a SYS8 [Section 3.5.8] which returns a pointer to the Current Process's support_t structure. This provides Support Level access to relevant *pcb* fields while hiding the Level 3 (and Level 2) *pcb* fields.

The SYS1 service is requested by the calling process by placing the value 1 in **a0**, a pointer to a processor state in **a1**, (optionally) a pointer to a Support Structure in **a2**, and then executing the **SYSCALL** instruction.

The following C code can be used to request a SYS1:

```
int retValue = SYSCALL (CREATEPROCESS,
        state_t *statep, support_t * supportp, 0);
```

Where the mnemonic constant CREATEPROCESS has the value of 1.

The newly populated *pcb* is placed on the Ready Queue and is made a child of the Current Process. Process Count is incremented by one, and control is returned to the Current Process. [Section 3.5.10]

In summary, for SYS1, one allocates a new *pcb* and initializes its fields:

- p_s from **a1**.

- p_supportStruct from **a2**. If no parameter is provided, this field is set to NULL.

- The *process queue* fields (e.g. p_next) by the call to insertProcQ

- The *process tree* fields (e.g. p_child) by the call to insertChild.

- p_time is set to zero; the new process has yet to accumulate any cpu time.

- p_semAdd is set to NULL; this *pcb*/process is in the "ready" state, not the "blocked" state.

3.5.2   Terminate_Process (SYS2)

This services causes the executing process to cease to exist. [Section 3.9] In addition, recursively, all progeny of this process are terminated as well. Execution of this instruction does not complete until *all* progeny are terminated, after which the Scheduler should be called.

The SYS2 service is requested by the calling process by placing the value 2 in **a0** and then executing the **SYSCALL** instruction.

The following C code can be used to request a SYS2:

```
SYSCALL (TERMINATEPROCESS, 0, 0, 0);
```

Where the mnemonic constant TERMINATEPROCESS has the value of 2.

3.5.3   Passeren (P) (SYS3)

This service requests the Nucleus to perform a P operation on a semaphore.

The P or SYS3 service is requested by the calling process by placing the value 3 in **a0**, the physical address of the semaphore to be P'ed in **a1**, and then executing the **SYSCALL** instruction.

Depending on the value of the semaphore, control is either returned to the Current Process, or this process is blocked on the ASL (transitions from "running" to "blocked") and the Scheduler is called.

The following C code can be used to request a SYS3:

```
SYSCALL (PASSEREN, int *semaddr, 0, 0);
```

Where the mnemonic constant PASSEREN has the value of 3.

3.5.4 Verhogen (V) (SYS4)

This service requests the Nucleus to perform a V operation on a semaphore.

The V or SYS4 service is requested by the calling process by placing the value 4 in **a0**, the physical address of the semaphore to be V'ed in **a1**, and then executing the **SYSCALL** instruction.

The following C code can be used to request a SYS4:

```
SYSCALL (VERHOGEN, int *semaddr, 0, 0);
```

Where the mnemonic constant VERHOGEN has the value of 4.

3.5.5 Wait_for_IO_Device (SYS5)

Pandos supports only synchronous I/O; an I/O operation is initiated, and the initiating process is blocked until the I/O completes. Whenever a process initiates an I/O operation, it will immediately issue a SYS5 for that device. Hence, a SYS5 is used to transition the Current Process from the "running" state to a "blocked" state.

More formally, this service performs a P operation on the semaphore that the Nucleus maintains for the I/O device indicated by the values in **a1**, **a2**, and optionally **a3**.

Since the semaphore that will have a P operation performed on it is a synchronization semaphore, this call should **always** block the Current Process on the ASL, after which the Scheduler is called.

Terminal devices are two independent sub-devices, and are handled by the SYS5 service as two independent devices. Hence each terminal device has two Nucleus maintained semaphores for it; one for character receipt and one for character transmission. [Section 5.7-*pops*]

As discussed below [Section 3.6], the Nucleus will perform a V operation on the Nucleus maintained semaphore whenever that (sub)device generates an interrupt.

Once the process resumes after the occurrence of the anticipated interrupt, the (sub)device's status word is returned in **v0**. For character transmission and receipt, the status word, in addition to containing a device completion code, will also contain the character transmitted or received.

The SYS5 service is requested by the calling process by placing the value 5 in **a0**, the interrupt line number in **a1** ([3...7]), the device number in **a2** ([0...7]), TRUE or FALSE in **a3** to indicate if waiting for a terminal read operation, and then executing the **SYSCALL** instruction.

The following C code can be used to request a SYS5:

```
int ioStatus = SYSCALL (WAITIO, int intlNo,
          int dnum, int waitForTermRead);
```

Where the mnemonic constant WAITIO has the value of 5.

3.5.6   Get_CPU_Time (SYS6)

This service requests that the accumulated processor time (in microseconds) used by the requesting process be placed/returned in the caller's **v0**. Hence, the Nucleus records (in the *pcb*: p_time) the amount of processor time used by each process. [Section 3.8]

The SYS6 service is requested by the calling process by placing the value 6 in **a0** and then executing the **SYSCALL** instruction.

The following C code can be used to request a SYS6:

```
cpu_t cpuTime = SYSCALL (GETCPUTIME, 0, 0, 0);
```

Where the mnemonic constant GETCPUTIME has the value of 6.

3.5.7 Wait_For_Clock (SYS7)

This service performs a P operation on the Nucleus maintained Pseudo-clock semaphore. This semaphore is V'ed every 100 milliseconds by the Nucleus. [Section 3.6.3]

Since the Pseudo-clock semaphore is a synchronization semaphore, this call should **always** block the Current Process on the ASL, after which the Scheduler is called. Hence, a SYS7 is used to transition the Current Process from the "running" state to a "blocked" state.

The SYS7 service is requested by the calling process by placing the value 7 in **a0** and then executing the **SYSCALL** instruction.

The following C code can be used to request a SYS7:

```
SYSCALL (WAITCLOCK, 0, 0, 0);
```

Where the mnemonic constant `WAITCLOCK` has the value of 7.

3.5.8 Get_SUPPORT_Data (SYS8)

This service requests a pointer to the Current Process's Support Structure. Hence, this service returns the value of `p_supportStruct` from the Current Process's *pcb*. If no value for `p_supportStruct` was provided for the Current Process when it was created, return NULL.

The SYS8 service is requested by the calling process by placing the value 8 in **a0** and then executing the **SYSCALL** instruction.

The following C code can be used to request a SYS6:

```
support_t *sPtr = SYSCALL (GETSUPPORTPTR, 0, 0, 0);
```

Where the mnemonic constant `GETSUPPORTPTR` has the value of 8.

3.5.9 SYS1-SYS8 in User-Mode

The above eight Nucleus services are considered privileged services and are only available to processes executing in kernel-mode. Any attempt to request one of these services while in user-mode should trigger a Program Trap exception response.

In particular the Nucleus should simulate a Program Trap exception when a privileged service is requested in user-mode. This is done by setting **Cause.ExcCode** in the stored exception state to *RI* (Reserved Instruction), and calling one's Program Trap exception handler.

Technical Point: As described above [Section 3.4], the saved exception state (for Processor 0) is stored at the start of the BIOS Data Page (0x0FFF.F000). [Section 3.2.2-*pops*]

3.5.10   Returning from a SYSCALL Exception

For **SYSCALL**s calls that do not block or terminate, control is returned to the Current Process at the conclusion of the Nucleus's **SYSCALL** exception handler. Observe that the correct processor state to load (**LDST**) is the saved exception state (located at the start of the BIOS Data Page [Section 3.4]) and not the obsolete processor state stored in the Current Process's *pcb*. The saved exception state was the state of the process at the time the **SYSCALL** was executed. The processor state in the Current Process's *pcb* was the state of the process at the start of it current time slice/quantum.

Hence, any return value described above (e.g. SYS6) needs to be put in the specified register in the stored exception state.

Furthermore, **SYSCALL**s that do not result in process termination (eventually) return control to the process's execution stream. This is done either immediately (e.g. SYS6) or after the process is blocked and eventually unblocked (e.g. SYS5). In any event the **PC** that was saved is, as it is for all exceptions, the address of the instruction that caused that exception – the address of the **SYSCALL** assembly instruction. Without intervention, returning control to the **SYSCALL** requesting process will result in an infinite loop of **SYSCALL**'s. To avoid this the **PC** must be incremented by 4 (i.e. the μMPS3 wordsize) prior to returning control to the interrupted execution stream. While the **PC** needs to be altered, there is no need, in this case, to make a parallel assignment to **t9**.

3.5.11   Blocking SYSCALLs

For **SYSCALL**s that block (SYS3, SYS5, and SYS7), a number of steps need to be performed:

- As described above [Section 3.5.10] the value of the **PC** must be incremented by 4 to avoid an infinite loop of **SYSCALL**s.

- The saved processor state (located at the start of the BIOS Data Page[Section 3.4]) must be copied into the Current Process's *pcb* (p_s).

- Update the accumulated CPU time for the Current Process. [Section 3.8]

- The Current Process is blocked on the ASL (insertBlocked), transitioning the process from the "running" state, to the "blocked" state.

- Call the Scheduler.

3.6 Interrupt Exception Handling

A device or timer interrupt occurs when either a previously initiated I/O request completes or when either a Processor Local Timer (PLT) or the Interval Timer makes a 0x0000.0000 $\Rightarrow$ 0xFFFF.FFFF transition.

Assuming that the (Processor 0) Pass Up Vector was properly initialized by the Nucleus as part of Nucleus initialization [Section 3.1], and that the Nucleus exception handler (fooBar) correctly decodes **Cause.ExcCode** [Section 3.4], control should be passed to one's Nucleus interrupt exception handler.

Which interrupt lines have pending interrupts is set in **Cause.IP**. [Section 3.3-*pops*] Furthermore, for interrupt lines 3–7 the Interrupting Devices Bit Map will indicate which devices on each of these interrupt lines have a pending interrupt. [Section 5.2.2-*pops*]

Since Pandos is intended for uniprocessor environments only, interrupt line 0 may safely be ignored. [Chapter 5-*pops*]

Note, many devices per interrupt line may have an interrupt request pending, and that many interrupt lines may simultaneously be on. Also, since each terminal device is two sub-devices, each terminal device may have two interrupts pending simultaneously as well. One should process only one interrupt at a time: the interrupt with the highest priority. The lower the interrupt line and device number, the higher the priority of the interrupt. When there are multiple interrupts pending, and the interrupt exception handler processes only the single highest priority pending interrupt, the interrupt exception handler will be immediately re-entered as soon as interrupts are unmasked again; effectively forming a loop until all the pending interrupts are processed.

Since terminal devices are actually two sub-devices, both sub-devices may have an interrupt pending simultaneously. For purposes of prioritizing pending interrupts, terminal transmission (i.e. writing to the terminal) is of higher priority than terminal receipt (i.e. reading from the terminal). Hence, the PLT (interrupt line 1) is the highest priority interrupt, while reading from terminal 7 (interrupt line 7, device 7; read) is the lowest priority interrupt.

The interrupt exception handler's first step is to determine which device or timer with an outstanding interrupt is the highest priority.

Depending on the device, the interrupt exception handler will perform a number of tasks.

3.6.1 Non-Timer Interrupts

1. Calculate the address for this device's device register. [Section 5.1-*pops*]

2. Save off the status code from the device's device register.

3. Acknowledge the outstanding interrupt. This is accomplished by writing the acknowledge command code in the interrupting device's device register. Alternatively, writing a new command in the interrupting device's device register will also acknowledge the interrupt.

4. Perform a V operation on the Nucleus maintained semaphore associated with this (sub)device. This operation should unblock the process (*pcb*) which initiated this I/O operation and then requested to wait for its completion via a SYS5 operation.

5. Place the stored off status code in the newly unblocked *pcb*'s **v0** register.

6. Insert the newly unblocked *pcb* on the Ready Queue, transitioning this process from the "blocked" state to the "ready" state.

7. Return control to the Current Process: Perform a **LDST** on the saved exception state (located at the start of the BIOS Data Page [Section 3.4]).

Important Point: It is possible that the V operation (increment the indicated semaphore and unblock a *pcb*) returns NULL instead of a *pcb*. This can happen if while waiting for the initiated I/O operation to complete, an ancestor of this *pcb* was terminated. In this case, simply return control to the Current Process.

Important Point: It is also possible that there is no Current Process to return control to. This will be the case when the Scheduler executes the **WAIT** instruction instead of dispatching a process for execution. [Section 3.2]

Technical Point: In μMPS3 it is technically feasible for a process to initiate an I/O operation and for the interrupt associated with this operation to occur *before* it has an opportunity to execute its SYS5. However, the Pandos specification for the Support Level prevents this from happening.

3.6.2 Processor Local Timer (PLT) Interrupts

The PLT is used to support CPU scheduling. The Scheduler will load the PLT with the value of 5 milliseconds whenever it dispatches a process. [Section 3.2]
  This "running" process will either:

- Terminate. Execute a SYS2 or cause an exception without having set a Support Structure address. [Section 3.7]

- Transition from the "running" state to the "blocked" state; execute a SYS3, SYS5, or SYS7.

- Be interrupted by a PLT interrupt.

The last option means that the Current Process has used up its time quantum/slice but has not completed its *CPU Burst*. Hence, it must be transitioned from the "running" state to the "ready" state.
  The PLT portion of the interrupt exception handler should therefore:

- Acknowledge the PLT interrupt by loading the timer with a new value. [Section 4.1.4-*pops*]

- Copy the processor state at the time of the exception (located at the start of the BIOS Data Page [Section 3.2.2-*pops*]) into the Current Process's *pcb* (p_s).

- Place the Current Process on the Ready Queue; transitioning the Current Process from the "running" state to the "ready" state.

- Call the Scheduler.

3.6.3   The System-wide Interval Timer and the Pseudo-clock

The *Pseudo-clock* is a facility provided by the Nucleus for the Support Level. The Nucleus promises to perform a V operation, every 100 milliseconds, on a special Nucleus maintained semaphore; the Pseudo-clock semaphore. [Section 3.1] This periodic V operation is called a *Pseudo-clock Tick*.

To perform a P operation on the Pseudo-clock semaphore (i.e. transition from the "running" state to the "blocked" state on this semaphore), the Current Process will perform a SYS7.

Since the Interval Timer is only used for this purpose, all line 2 interrupts indicate that it is time to P the Pseudo-clock semaphore; a Pseudo-clock tick.

The Interval Timer portion of the interrupt exception handler should therefore:

1. Acknowledge the interrupt by loading the Interval Timer with a new value: 100 milliseconds. [Section 4.1.3-*pops*]

2. Unblock **ALL** *pcb*s blocked on the Pseudo-clock semaphore. Hence, the semantics of this semaphore are a bit different than traditional synchronization semaphores

3. Reset the Pseudo-clock semaphore to zero. This insures that all SYS7 calls block and that the Pseudo-clock semaphore does not grow positive.

4. Return control to the Current Process: Perform a **LDST** on the saved exception state (located at the start of the BIOS Data Page [Section 3.4]).

Important Point: It is also possible that there is no Current Process to return control to. This will be the case when the Scheduler executes the **WAIT** instruction instead of dispatching a process for execution. [Section 3.2]

3.7   Pass Up or Die

The Nucleus will directly handle all SYS1-SYS8 requests and device (internal timers and peripheral devices) interrupts. For all other exceptions (e.g. **SYSCALL** exceptions numbered 9 and above, Program Trap and TLB exceptions) the Nucleus will take one of two actions depending on whether the offending process (i.e. the Current Process) was provided a non-NULL value for its Support Structure pointer when it was created. [Section 3.5.1]

- If the Current Process's p_supportStruct is NULL, then the exception should be handled as a SYS2: the Current Process and all its progeny are terminated. This is the "die" portion of Pass Up or Die.

- If the Current Process's p_supportStruct is non-NULL. The handling of the exception is "passed up."

When an exception occurs, the processor, in concert with the BIOS-Excpt handler, "passes up" the handling of the exception to the Nucleus: store the saved exception state at an accessible location known to the Nucleus, and pass control to a routine specified by the Nucleus, i.e. the Nucleus Exception handler (fooBar).

- The location, in this case, is fixed; a given location in the BIOS Data Page. (For Processor 0, this is 0x0FFF.F000) [Section 3.2.2-*pops*]

- The address (and stack pointer) for the handler to pass control to was seeded by the Nucleus, during Nucleus initialization, in the appropriate location of the Pass Up Vector. [Section 3.1]

When the Nucleus "passes up" exception handling to the Support Level, it essentially performs the same two tasks: copy the saved exception state into a location accessible to the Support Level, and pass control to a routine specified by the Support Level.

There is only one location for the saved exception state and one Pass Up Vector for the Nucleus. This is because the Nucleus runs in single threaded mode with interrupts masked; hence with no concurrency. The Nucleus services run in a "one at a time" mode, and each invocation running to completion without interruption. Hence the reusability of the BIOS Data Page location for the saved exception state and Pass Up Vector. This is also why Nucleus services are so limited: do only what must be done in single threaded mode, and pass up the handling of all other service requests.

Since the Support Level runs in a fully concurrent mode (interrupts unmasked), each process needs its own location(s) for their saved exception states, and addresses to pass control to: The Support Structure.

Furthermore, the concurrency at the Support Level is not only inter-process, but intra-process as well. The Support Level, while handling a passed up **SYSCALL**, can trigger a page fault. For this reason, the Support Structure contains **two** locations for saved exception states, and two addresses for handlers. One state_t/PC address pair for:

- TLB exceptions (i.e. page faults): The Support Level TLB exception handler.

- All other exceptions: The Support Level general exception handler.

One last important detail. The Support Structure's version of a Pass Up Vector needs to contain three register values and not two. In addition to the **PC/SP**, one also needs a new value for the **Status** register.

A **PC/SP/Status** combination is also referred to as a *context*. Hence the Support Structure's version of a Pass Up Vector needs to store two processor context sets: one for non-TLB exceptions and one for TLB exceptions.

The following two structures are provided:

```
/* process context */
typedef struct context_t {
    /* process context fields */
    unsigned int c_stackPtr,           /* stack pointer value */
                 c_status,             /* status reg value    */
                 c_pc;                 /* PC address          */
} context_t;

typedef struct support_t {
    int          sup_asid;             /* Process Id (asid)   */
    state_t      sup_exceptState[2];   /* stored excpt states */
    context_t    sup_exceptContext[2]; /* pass up contexts    */
    ... other fields to be added later
} support_t;

 /* Exceptions related constants */
#define PGFAULTEXCEPT 0
#define GENERALEXCEPT 1
```

To pass up the handling of an exception:

- Copy the saved exception state from the BIOS Data Page to the correct sup_exceptState field of the Current Process. The Current Process's *pcb* should point to a non-null support_t.

- Perform a **LDCXT** using the fields from the correct sup_exceptContext field of the Current Process. [Section 7.3.4-*pops*]

3.7.1   SYSCALL Exceptions Numbered 9 and Above

A **SYSCALL** exception numbered 9 and above occurs when the Current Process executes the **SYSCALL** instruction (**Cause.ExcCode** is set to 8 [Section 3.4]) and the contents of **a0** is greater than or equal to 9.

The Nucleus **SYSCALL** exception handler should perform a standard Pass Up or Die operation using the GENERALEXCEPT index value.

3.7.2   Program Trap Exception Handling

A Program Trap exception occurs when the Current Process attempts to perform some illegal or undefined action. A Program Trap exception is defined as an exception with **Cause.ExcCode**s of 4-7, 9-12. [Section 3.4]

The Nucleus Program Trap exception handler should perform a standard Pass Up or Die operation using the GENERALEXCEPT index value.

3.7.3   TLB Exception Handling

A TLB exception occurs when μMPS3 fails in an attempt to translate a logical address into its corresponding physical address. A TLB exception is defined as an exception with **Cause.ExcCode**s of 1-3. [Section 3.4]

The Nucleus TLB exception handler should perform a standard Pass Up or Die operation using the PGFAULTEXCEPT index value.

3.8   Accumulated CPU Time

μMPS3 has three clocks: the TOD clock, Interval Timer, and the PLT, though only the Interval Timer and the PLT can generate interrupts. This fits nicely with two of three primary timing needs:

- Generate an interrupt to signal the end of Current Process's time quantum/slice. The PLT is reserved for this purpose.

- Generate Pseudo-clock ticks: Cause an interrupt to occur every 100 milliseconds and V the Pseudo-clock semaphore. The Interval Timer is reserved for this purpose.

The third timing need is that the Nucleus is tasked with keeping track of the accumulated CPU time used by each process. [Section 3.5.6]

A field has been defined in the *pcb* for this purpose (p_time). Hence SYS6 should return the value in the Current Process's p_time *plus* the amount of CPU time used during the current quantum/time slice. While the TOD clock does not generate interrupts, it is, however, well suited for keeping track of an interval's length.

By storing off the TOD clock's value at both the start and end of an interval, one can compute the duration of that interval. [Section 4.1.2-*pops*]

The three timer devices are mechanisms for implementing Pandos's policies. Timing policy questions that need to be worked out include:

- While the time spent by the Nucleus handling an I/O or Interval Timer interrupt needs to be measured for Pseudo-clock tick purposes, which process, if any, should be "charged" with this time? Note: it is possible for an I/O or Interval Timer interrupt to occur even when there is no Current Process.

- While the time spent by the Nucleus handling a **SYSCALL** request needs to be measured for Pseudo-clock tick and quantum/time slice purposes, which process, if any, should be "charged" with this time?

It is important to understand the functional differences between the three μMPS3 timer devices. This includes, but is not limited to understanding that the TOD clock counts up while the other two timers count down, and that the behavior of the PLT differs from that of the Interval Timer. The PLT can be enabled/disabled via the processor Local Timer enable bit (**Status.TE**). [Section 4.1.4-*pops*]

3.9 Process Termination

When a process is terminated (SYS2 or the "Die" portion of Pass Up or Die) there is actually a whole (sub)tree of processes that get terminated. There are a number of tasks that must be accomplished:

- The root of the sub-tree of terminated processes must be "orphaned" from its parents; its parent can no longer have this *pcb* as one of its progeny (out_Child).

- If the value of a semaphore is negative, it is an invariant that the absolute value of the semaphore equal the number of *pcb*'s blocked on that semaphore. Hence if a terminated process is blocked on a semaphore, the value of the semaphore must be adjusted; i.e. incremented.

- If a terminated process is blocked on a device semaphore, the semaphore should NOT be adjusted. When the interrupt eventually occurs the semaphore will get V'ed (and hence incremented) by the interrupt handler.

- The process count and soft-blocked variables need to be adjusted accordingly.

- Processes (i.e. *pcb*'s) can't hide. A *pcb* is either the Current Process ("running"), sitting on the Ready Queue ("ready"), blocked on a device semaphore ("blocked"), or blocked on a non-device semaphore ("blocked").

3.10 Nuts and Bolts

3.10.1 Module Decomposition

One possible module decomposition is as follows:

1. initial.c This module implements `main()` and exports the Nucleus's global variables. (e.g. process count, device semaphores, etc.)

2. interrupts.c This module implements the device/timer interrupt exception handler. This module will process all the device/timer interrupts, converting device/timer interrupts into V operations on the appropriate semaphores.

3. exceptions.c This module implements the TLB, Program Trap, and **SYSCALL** exception handlers. Furthermore, this module will contain the provided skeleton TLB-Refill event handler (e.g. `uTLB_RefillHandler`).

4. scheduler.c This module implements the Scheduler and the deadlock detector.

3.10.2 Accessing the `libumps` Library

Accessing the **CP0** registers and the BIOS-implemented services/instructions in C (e.g. **WAIT, LDST**) is via the `libumps` library. [Chapter 7-*pops*]
Simply include the line

```
#include ``/usr/include/umps3/umps/libumps.h''
```

in one's source files.[1]

3.11   Testing

There is a provided test file, **p2test.c** that will "exercise" your code. [Appendix A]

As with any non-trivial system, you are strongly encouraged to use the *make* program to maintain your code. A sample *Makefile* has been supplied. See Chapter 10 in the POPS reference for more compilation details.

Once your (seven?) source files (two from Phase 1 and four from Phase 2) have been correctly compiled, linked together (with appropriate linker script, `crtso.o`, and `libumps.o`), and post-processed with **umps3-elf2umps** (all performed by the sample *Makefile*), your code can be tested by launching the μMPS3 emulator. At a terminal prompt, enter:

> umps3

The **p2test.c** code assumes that the TLB Floor Address has been set to any value except **VM OFF**. The value of the TLB Floor Address is a user configurable value set via the μMPS3 Machine Configuration Panel. [Chapter 12]

The test program reports on its progress by writing messages to TERMINAL0. At the conclusion of the test program, either successful or unsuccessful, μMPS3 will display a final message and then enter an infinite loop. The final message will either be **System Halted** for successful termination, or **Kernel Panic** for unsuccessful termination.

---

[1]The file libumps.h is part of the μMPS3 distribution. /usr/include/umps3/umps/ is the recommended installation location for this file.

If you want to travel around the world and be invited to speak at a lot of different places, just write a Unix operating system.

Linus Torvalds

Phase 3 - Level 4: The Support Level

Level 4, the Support Level, builds on the Nucleus in two key ways to create an environment for the execution of user-processes (U-proc's):

- Support for address translation/virtual memory. Each U-proc will execute in its own identically structured logical address space (**kuseg**), with a unique Address space identifiers (i.e. process ID), **ASID**. [Section 6.2-*pops*]

- Support for character-oriented I/O devices: terminals and printers. Each U-proc is assigned its own printer and terminal.

Specifically, the Support Level provides the exception handlers that the Nucleus "passes" handling "up" to; assuming the process was provided a non-NULL value for its Support Structure. [Section 3.7]

There will be one Level 4/Phase 3 exception handler for:

- TLB Management (TLB) exceptions: The Support Level page fault handler, i.e. the Pager. [Section 4.4]

- non-TLB exceptions. This hander is for all SYSCALL (**SYSCALL**) exceptions numbered 9 and above, and all Program Trap exceptions. [Section 4.6]

41

These two exception handlers will run in kernel-mode with interrupts enabled, while the U-proc's will run in user-mode, with interrupts enabled. Hence each U-proc leads a schizophrenic life; mostly executing in user-mode, but sometimes, after the handling of an exception is "passed" back up to it; executing in kernel-mode. While the Nucleus exception and interrupt handlers are system-wide resources that all processes share (in serial fashion with interrupts disabled), the Support Level exception handlers are more like Support Level provided libraries that becomes part of each U-proc.[1]

Finally, instead of using the Nucleus's test program (`test`) place holder TLB-Refill event handler (`uTLB_RefillHandler`), the Support Level will implement its own TLB-Refill event handler. [Section 4.3]

Hence, the bulk of this phase is the implementation of these three exception event handlers.

4.1   Address Translation: The OS Perspective

Before getting into how Pandos supports address translation, one must fully understand how the μMPS3 hardware supports address translation. [Chapter 6-*pops*] & [Figure 6.9-*pops*]

Essentially, every logical address for which translation is called for (any address above the TLB Floor Address) triggers a hardware search of the TLB seeking a *matching* TLB entry. If no matching entry is found a TLB-Refill event is triggered. Assuming the Nucleus correctly initialized the Processor 0 Pass Up Vector with the address of the TLB-Refill event handler [Section 3.1], control should continue with the Support Level's TLB-Refill event handler. (e.g. `uTLB_RefillHandler`) This function will locate the correct Page Table entry in some Support Level data structure (i.e. a U-proc's *Page Table*), write it into the TLB (**TLBWR** or **TLBWI** [Section 6.4-*pops*] & [Section 4.5.2]), and return control (**LDST**) to the Current Process to restart the address translation process.

Once a matching TLB entry is found and it is marked *valid*, the μMPS3 hardware constructs the corresponding physical address. If the matching TLB entry is marked *invalid*, or the access represents an attempt to modify memory and the matching TLB entry's **D** bit is off, a TLB exception is raised: TLB-Invalid or

---

[1]Technically, this is not true for the TLB-Refill event handler (e.g. `uTLB_RefillHandler`) which will behave like a Nucleus exception handler - a system-wide resource that all processes will share in serial fashion. However, since it is a part of the address translation process, it is included as part of Level 4/Phase 3.

TLB-Modification. The Support Level TLB exception handler will handle TLB-Invalid exceptions, i.e. page faults. [Section 4.4]
Since all Page Table entries (and therefore all TLB entries) should be marked as *dirty* (the **D** bit on), TLB-Modification exceptions should not occur.

This implies the following Support Level data structures:

- One Page Table per U-proc. A Pandos Page Table will be an array of 32 Page Table entries. Each Page Table entry is a doubleword consisting of an **EntryHi** and an **EntryLo** portion. [Section 6.3.2-*pops*] This array should be added to the Support Structure (support_t) that is pointed to by a U-proc's *pcb*. [Section 3.7]

  Technical Point: TLB entries and Page Table entries are identical in structure: a doubleword consisting of an **EntryHi** and an **EntryLo** portion. Which term is used will be dependent on context.

- The *Swap Pool*; a set of RAM frames reserved for virtual memory. Logical pages will occupy these frames when present. The size of the Swap Pool should be set to two times UPROCMAX, where UPROCMAX is defined as the specific degree of multiprogramming to be supported: [1...8]. The Swap Pool is not so much a Support Level data structure, but a set of RAM frames reserved to support paging.

- The Swap Pool data structure/table. The Support Level will maintain a table, one entry per Swap Pool frame, recording information about the logical page occupying it. At a minimum, each entry should record the **ASID** and logical page number of the occupying page.

- The Swap Pool semaphore. A mutual exclusion semaphore (hence initialized to 1) that controls access to the Swap Pool data structure.

- Backing store; secondary storage that contains each U-proc's complete logical image – which for Pandos is limited to 32 pages in size. Associated with each U-proc is a flash device which will be configured (preloaded) to contain that U-proc's logical image. While slightly unrealistic, this *basic* version of the Support Level will use each U-proc's flash device as its backing store device.

4.2   A U-proc's Logical Address Space and Backing Store

Each U-proc *executes* in the **kuseg** address space [Section 6.2-*pops*], in user-mode, with interrupts enabled, and a unique **ASID** value.

ASID 0 is reserved for kernel daemons, so the (up to) eight U-proc's should be assigned **ASID** values from [1..8].

The first page, for each U-proc is 0x8000.0000. The second page is 0x8000.1000, and so on. A Pandos U-proc's **.text** and **.data** regions, together can be no larger than 31 pages. (0x8001.E000).

The stack page is limited to one page and is set to the halfway point in **kuseg**. The **SP** will start at 0xC000.0000 and grow downward. Pandos, does not support dynamic variables, hence there is no heap space.

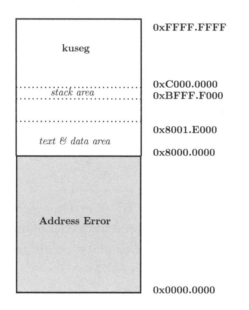

Figure 4.1: Layout of a U-proc inside **kuseg**

When a process is initiated, an operating system would typically read the contents of the executable file (e.g. *.aout* file) and use its contents to:

- Set up the new process's Page Table; which would reflect that none of the process's pages are *present*.

- Set up the new process's backing store on a secondary storage device.

4.2.1 A U-proc's Page Table

While the μMPS3 hardware defines the structure of a TLB entry, it does not define the structure of a Page Table. A μMPS3-compatible operating system is free to define a Page Table however it wishes; the hardware never interacts directly with Page Tables, just with the TLB.

When a TLB-Refill event occurs, the operating system builds an appropriate TLB entry from the data in a Page Table and writes the entry into the TLB. To simply this process, Pandos defines a Page Table entry to be identical to a TLB entry. Hence, in Pandos, a Page Table is an array of TLB entries.

Each U-proc's Page Table will be an array of 32 TLB entries. (Or equivalently, an array of 32 Page Table entries.) The first 31 entries are for the **.text** and **.data** pages of the logical address space. (Logical page number 0 through page number 30, starting from 0x8000.0000.) The final entry is for the U-proc's stack page. (Logical page number 0x3FFF.F000, starting from 0x8000.0000.)

	EntryHI			EntryLo	
	VPN	ASID		PFN	N D V G
0	0x80000	i			1:0
1	0x80001	i			1:0
·					
·					
·					
30	0x8001E	i			1:0
31	0xBFFFF	i			1:0

Figure 4.2: Layout of U-proc i's Page Table

To initialize a Page Table one needs to set the **VPN**, **ASID**, **V**, and **D** bit fields for each Page Table entry. [Section 6.3.2-*pops*]

- The **VPN** field will be set to [0x80000..0x8001E] for the first 31 entries. The **VPN** for the stack page (Page Table entry 31) should be set to 0xBFFFF - the starting address whose top end is 0xC000.0000. (The value that **SP** is initialized to.)

- The **ASID** field, for any given Page Table, will all be set to the U-proc's unique ID: an integer from [1..8]

- The **D** bit field will be set to 1 (on) - each page is write-enabled.

- The **G** bit field will be set to 1 (off) - these pages are private to the specific **ASID**.

- The **V** bit field will be set to 0 (off) - the entry is NOT valid. i.e. A copy of this page is not also currently residing in RAM.

4.2.2   A U-proc's Backing Store

Since there is no file system (yet) containing files (executable or otherwise, e.g. *.aout*), which the operating system would read to set up both the Page Table and the backing store, the supplied utility umps3-mkdev [Section 11.2-*pops*] can be configured to preload a flash device with the contents of a *.aout* file in a manner that makes it suitable to be used as that process's backing store.

Hence, user processes are not represented by a file to be processed (i.e. initialize a Page Table and set up the backing store), but via individual secondary storage devices (flash device) each preconfigured/already initialized with that process's logical image/backing store data.

Specifically, each U-proc will be associated with a unique flash device, preloaded with that process's logical image, which the Support Level will then use as the process's backing store device.

4.3   The TLB-Refill event handler

When a logical address translation's search of the of the TLB for a *matching* entry fails, a TLB-Refill event is triggered. Assuming the Nucleus correctly initialized the Processor 0 Pass Up Vector with the address of the TLB-Refill event handler [Section 3.1], control should continue with the Pandos TLB-Refill event handler. (e.g. uTLB_RefillHandler)

A TLB-Refill event is essentially a cache-miss event since the TLB is a cache of the most recently executed processes' Page Table entries. It is the job of the TLB-Refill event handler to insert into the TLB the missing Page Table entry and restart the instruction.

The Level 3/Phase 2 Nucleus code implemented a skeleton TLB-Refill event handler (e.g. uTLB_RefillHandler). [Section 3.3] The supplied skeleton code should, as part of this phase, be replaced (inplace) with the code for an actual TLB-Refill event handler.

Technical Point: The TLB-Refill event handler is actually a Level 3/Phase 2 handler in that it executes in kernel-mode, with interrupts disabled, and uses the first frame of RAM as its stack page; the Nucleus stack page [Section 3.1]. As such, like the other Level 3/Phase2 handlers (and unlike all the other Level 4/Phase 3 exception handlers) it is allowed access to the Level 3/Phase 2 global structures. (e.g. Current Process) However, since it is a key component in Pandos's implementation of virtual memory, its implementation is part of Level 4/Phase 3, and therefore also has access to a process's Support Structure (e.g. the Page Table).

This function will:

- Locate the correct Page Table entry in the Current Process's Page Table; a component of `p_supportStruct` [Section 3.7]

- Write the entry into the TLB using the **TLBWR** instruction. [Section 6.4-*pops*]).

- Return control (**LDST**) to the Current Process to restart the address translation process.

To accomplish this, a TLB-Refill event handler must:

1. Determine the page number (denoted as p) of the missing TLB entry by inspecting **EntryHi** in the saved exception state located at the start of the BIOS Data Page. [Section 3.4]

2. Get the Page Table entry for page number p for the Current Process. This will be located in the Current Process's Page Table, which is part of its Support Structure.

3. Write this Page Table entry into the TLB. This is a three-set process:

    (a) **setENTRYHI**
    (b) **setENTRYLO**
    (c) **TLBWR**

4. Return control to the Current Process to retry the instruction that caused the TLB-Refill event: **LDST** on the saved exception state located at the start of the BIOS Data Page.

4.4   Paging in Pandos

4.4.1   The Swap Pool

A *Swap Pool* is a set of RAM frames set aside to support virtual memory. To ensure the proper exercise of Pandos's paging functionality, the size of the Swap Pool should be set to two times UPROCMAX, where UPROCMAX is defined as the specific degree of multiprogramming to be supported/implemented: [1...8]. (i.e. The number of U-procs to be concurrently executed.)

The Swap Pool can be placed anywhere in unused RAM: from the end of the operating system code, to the start of the last frame of RAM (which Level 3/Phase 2 allocated as the stack page for the initial process - test).

The recommended location in Pandos is to place the Swap Pool after the end of the operating system code. Though the size of one's operating system code is unknown,[2] simply overestimate its size. For example, assume one's Pandos code base (plus Nucleus stack) occupies no more than 32 frames. Hence, the Swap Pool's starting address is: 0x2002.0000 (0x2000.0000 + (32 * PAGESIZE))

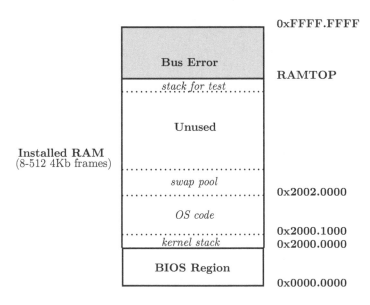

Figure 4.3: Memory Layout for the Swap Pool

---

[2]The operating system object format, *.core* is a variant of the *.aout* format. The header information in both a *.core* and *.aout* file contains information describing the size of the code (**.text** and **.data**). [Section 10.3.1-*pops*]

Important Point: Using the μMPS3 Machine Configuration Panel make sure that there is sufficient "installed" RAM for the OS code, the Swap Pool and stack page for `test`. [Section 12.2.1-*pops*]

The Support Level must maintain a table, one entry per frame in the Swap Pool, recording information about the logical page occupying it. This table should be composed of three columns/fields:

1. The **ASID** of the U-proc whose page is occupying the frame.

2. The logical page number (**VPN**) of the occupying page.

3. A pointer to the matching Page Table entry in the Page Table belonging to the owner process. (i.e. **ASID**)

Technical Point: Since all valid **ASID** values are positive numbers, one can indicate that a frame is unoccupied with an entry of -1 in that frame's **ASID** entry in the Swap Pool table.

The size of the table must match the size of the Swap Pool: one entry per frame in the Swap Pool.

Finally, the Swap Pool table is a shared data structure that must be accessed or updated in a mutually exclusive manner. Hence, the Support Level will also define a mutual exclusion semaphore (the Swap Pool semaphore) to control access to the Swap Pool table. To access the Swap Pool table, a process must first perform a SYS3 (P) operation on this semaphore. When access to the Swap Pool table is concluded, a process will then perform a SYS4 (V) operation on this semaphore. Since this semaphore is used for mutual exclusion, it should be initialized to one.

4.4.2 The Pager

While TLB-Refill events will be handled by the Support Level's TLB-Refill event handler (e.g. `uTLB_RefillHandler`), page faults are passed up by the Nucleus to the Support Level's TLB exception handler – the Pager.

μMPS3 defines three different TLB exceptions [Chapter 3-*pops*]:

- Page fault on a load operation: TLB-Invalid exception – *TLBL*

- Page fault on a store operation: TLB-Invalid exception – *TLBS*

- An attempted write to a read-only page: TLB-Modification exception – *Mod*

In Pandos, Page Table entries are to be marked as read-writable, therefore TLB-Modification exceptions should not occur. If they do, they should be treated as a program trap. [Section 4.8]

To handle a page fault, a Pandos TLB exception handler should perform the following steps:

1. Obtain the pointer to the Current Process's Support Structure: SYS8.

   Important Point: Level 4/Phase 3 exception handlers are limited in their interaction with the Nucleus and its data structures to the functionality of **SYSCALL**s [1..8]

2. Determine the cause of the TLB exception. The saved exception state responsible for this TLB exception should be found in the Current Process's Support Structure for TLB exceptions. (`sup_exceptState[0]`'s **Cause** register)

3. If the **Cause** is a TLB-Modification exception, treat this exception as a program trap [Section 4.8], otherwise continue.

4. Gain mutual exclusion over the Swap Pool table. (SYS3 – P operation on the Swap Pool semaphore)

5. Determine the missing page number (denoted as p): found in the saved exception state's **EntryHi**.

6. Pick a frame, i, from the Swap Pool. Which frame is selected is determined by the Pandos page replacement algorithm. [Section 4.5.4]

7. Determine if frame i is occupied; examine entry i in the Swap Pool table.

8. If frame i is currently occupied, assume it is occupied by logical page number k belonging to process x (**ASID**) and that it is "dirty" (i.e. been modified):

(a) Update process x's Page Table: mark Page Table entry k as not valid. This entry is easily accessible, since the Swap Pool table's entry i contains a pointer to this Page Table entry.

(b) Update the TLB, if needed. The TLB is a cache of the most recently executed process's Page Table entries. If process x's page k's Page Table entry is currently cached in the TLB it is clearly out of date; it was just updated in the previous step.

Important Point: This step and the previous step must be accomplished atomically. [Section 4.5.3]

(c) Update process x's backing store. Write the contents of frame i to the correct location on process x's backing store/flash device. [Section 4.5.1]

Treat any error status from the write operation as a program trap. [Section 4.8]

9. Read the contents of the Current Process's backing store/flash device logical page p into frame i. [Section 4.5.1]
Treat any error status from the read operation as a program trap. [Section 4.8]

10. Update the Swap Pool table's entry i to reflect frame i's new contents: page p belonging to the Current Process's **ASID**, and a pointer to the Current Process's Page Table entry for page p.

11. Update the Current Process's Page Table entry for page p to indicate it is now present (**V** bit) and occupying frame i (**PFN** field).

12. Update the TLB. The cached entry in the TLB for the Current Process's page p is clearly out of date; it was just updated in the previous step.

Important Point: This step and the previous step must be accomplished atomically. [Section 4.5.3]

13. Release mutual exclusion over the Swap Pool table. (SYS4 – V operation on the Swap Pool semaphore)

14. Return control to the Current Process to retry the instruction that caused the page fault: **LDST** on the saved exception state.

4.5   Miscellaneous Details Related to Paging

4.5.1   Reading and Writing from/to a Flash Device

μMPS3 flash devices are highly abstracted versions of real flash devices. It is convenient to think of them as isomorphic to seek-less, 1-dimensional disk devices. Flash device blocks are numbered sequentially [0..**MAXBLOCK**-1]. To read/write a flash device one performs the following two steps in order [Section 5.4-*pops*]:

1. Write the flash device's **DATA0** field with the appropriate starting physical address of the 4k block to be read (or written); the particular frame's starting address.

2. Write the flash device's **COMMAND** field with the device block number (high order three bytes) and the command to read (or write) in the lower order byte.

As with all I/O operations, this should be immediately followed by a SYS5. [Section 3.5.5]

Important Point: To insure that the interrupt always happens **after** the SYS5, one should write the **COMMAND** field and issue the SYS5 atomically. [Section 4.11.1]

Each U-proc is associated with its own flash device, already initialized with its backing store data. [Section 4.2.2] The flash device's blocks [0..30] will used store the U-proc's **.text**, and **.data**, while block 31 will hold the U-proc's stack page.

4.5.2   Updating the TLB

The TLB is a cache of Page Table entries across multiple U-proc's. Hence, whenever a Page Table entry is updated by the Pager, if that entry is also present/cached in the TLB, there is a cache consistency problem. There are two approaches one can employ to guarantee cache consistency. [Section 6.4-*pops*]

The two approaches are:

- Probe the TLB (**TLBP**) to see if the newly updated TLB entry is indeed cached in the TLB. If so (**Index.P** is 0), rewrite (update) that entry (**TLBWI**) to match the entry in the Page Table.

- Erase ALL the entries in the TLB (**TLBCLR**).

While the first approach is the recommended approach for Pandos. One should initially implement the second approach and then refactor to employ the first approach after all other aspects of the Support Level are completed/debugged.

4.5.3 Updating a Page Table and the TLB Atomically

The order of operations for the Pager are important. Specifically:

- When refreshing the backing store, one must first update the Page Table, and possibly the TLB, *before* performing the write operation.

- When reading in from the backing store, one must first perform the read operation *before* updating the Page Table and TLB.

Thought Challenge: Why must these operations be done in the prescribed order?

Similarly, the updating of a Page Table entry and its cached counterpart in the TLB, must be done atomically. This is accomplished in μMPS3 by disabling interrupts before the update statements, and then reenabling them immediately afterwards. Interrupts are disabled and enabled via the **STATUS** register (**setSTATUS**). [Section 7.1-*pops*]

Thought Challenge: Why must the Page Table and TLB be updated atomically?

4.5.4 The Pandos Page Replacement Algorithm

When a page fault occurs, the page replacement algorithm picks one of the frames from the Swap Pool. The recommended Pandos page replacement algorithm is *First in First out*.

Though inefficient, this "round robin" algorithm is easily implemented via a `static` variable. Whenever a frame is needed to support a page fault, simply increment this variable `mod` the size of the Swap Pool.

4.6 The Support Level General Exception Handler

The Support Level general exception handler will process all passed up non-TLB exceptions:

- All SYSCALL (**SYSCALL**) exceptions numbered 9 and above.

- All Program Trap exceptions; all exception causes exclusive of those for **SYSCALL** exceptions and those related to TLB exceptions. [Section 3.7.2]

Assuming that the handling of the exception is to be passed up (non-NULL Support Structure pointer) and the appropriate `sup_exceptContext` fields of the Support Structure were correctly initialized, execution continues with the Support Level's general exception handler. The processor state at the time of the exception will be in the Support Structure's corresponding `sup_exceptState` field. [Section 3.7]

After examining the `sup_exceptState`'s **Cause** register, the Support Level general exception hander will pass control to either the Support Level's **SYSCALL** exception handler [Section 4.7], or the Support Level's Program Trap exception handler. [Section 4.8]

4.7   The SYSCALL Exception Handler

The nucleus directly handles all SYS1-SYS8 **SYSCALL** exceptions. For all other **SYSCALL** exceptions the nucleus either treats the exception as a SYS2 (terminate) or "passes up" the handling of the exception if the offending process was provided a non-NULL value for its Support Structure pointer when it was created. [Section 3.7]

Assuming that the handling of the exception is to be passed up (non-NULL Support Structure pointer) and the appropriate `sup_exceptContext` fields of the Support Structure were correctly initialized, execution continues with the Support Level's general exception handler, which should then pass control to the Support Level's **SYSCALL** exception handler. The processor state at the time of the exception will be in the Support Structure's corresponding `sup_exceptState` field. [Section 3.7]

By convention the executing process places appropriate values in the general purpose registers **a0–a3** immediately prior to executing the **SYSCALL** instruction. The Support Level's **SYSCALL** exception handler will then perform some service on behalf of the U-proc executing the **SYSCALL** instruction depending on the value found in **a0**.

Upon successful completion of a **SYSCALL** request any return status is placed in **v0**, and control is returned to the calling process at the instruction immediately following the **SYSCALL** instruction. Similar to what the Nucleus does when returning from a successful **SYSCALL** request [Section 3.5.10], the Support Level's **SYSCALL** exception handler must also increment the **PC** by 4 in order to return control to the instruction *after* the **SYSCALL** instruction.

In particular, if a U-proc executes a **SYSCALL** instruction and **a0** contained a value in the range [9..13] then the Support Level should perform one of the services described below.

4.7.1 Terminate (SYS9)

This services causes the executing U-proc to cease to exist. The SYS9 service is essentially a user-mode "wrapper" for the kernel-mode restricted SYS2 service.

The SYS9 service is requested by the calling process by placing the value 9 in **a0** and then executing a **SYSCALL** instruction.

The following C code can be used to request a SYS9:

```
SYSCALL (TERMINATE, 0, 0, 0);
```

Where the mnemonic constant TERMINATE has the value of 9.

4.7.2 Get_TOD (SYS10)

When this service is requested, it causes the number of microseconds since the system was last booted/reset to be placed/returned in the U-proc's **v0** register.

The SYS10 service is requested by the calling U-proc by placing the value 10 in **a0** and then executing a **SYSCALL** instruction.

The following C code can be used to request a SYS10:

```
unsigned int retValue = SYSCALL (GETTOD, 0, 0, 0);
```

Where the mnemonic constant GETTOD has the value of 10.

4.7.3 Write_To_Printer (SYS11)

When requested, this service causes the requesting U-proc to be suspended until a line of output (string of characters) has been transmitted to the printer device associated with the U-proc.

Once the process resumes, the number of characters actually transmitted is returned in **v0**.

The SYS11 service is requested by the calling U-proc by placing the value 11 in **a0**, the virtual address of the first character of the string to be transmitted in **a1**, the length of this string in **a2**, and then executing a **SYSCALL** instruction. Once the process resumes, the number of characters actually transmitted is returned in **v0** if the write was successful. If the operation ends with a status other than "Device Ready" (1), the negative of the device's status value is returned in **v0**.

It is an error to write to a printer device from an address outside of the requesting U-proc's logical address space, request a SYS11 with a length less than 0, or a length greater than 128. Any of these errors should result in the U-proc being terminated (SYS9).

The following C code can be used to request a SYS11:

```
int retValue = SYSCALL (WRITEPRINTER, char *virtAddr,
        int len, 0);
```

Where the mnemonic constant `WRITEPRINTER` has the value of 11.

4.7.4   Write_To_Terminal (SYS12)

When requested, this service causes the requesting U-proc to be suspended until a line of output (string of characters) has been transmitted to the terminal device associated with the U-proc.

The SYS12 service is requested by the calling U-proc by placing the value 12 in **a0**, the virtual address of the first character of the string to be transmitted in **a1**, the length of this string in **a2**, and then executing a **SYSCALL** instruction. Once the process resumes, the number of characters actually transmitted is returned in **v0** if the write was successful. If the operation ends with a status other than "Character Transmitted" (5), the negative of the device's status value is returned in **v0**.

It is an error to write to a terminal device from an address outside of the requesting U-proc's logical address space, request a SYS12 with a length less than 0, or a length greater than 128. Any of these errors should result in the U-proc being terminated (SYS9).

The following C code can be used to request a SYS12:

```
int retValue = SYSCALL (WRITETERMINAL, char *virtAddr,
        int len, 0);
```

Where the mnemonic constant `WRITETERMINAL` has the value of 12.

4.7.5   Read_From_Terminal (SYS13)

`int SYS12 (READ_FROM_TERMINAL, char *addr)` When requested, this service causes the requesting U-proc to be suspended until a line of input (string of characters) has been transmitted from the terminal device associated with the U-proc.

The SYS13 service is requested by the calling U-proc by placing the value 13 in **a0**, the virtual address of a string buffer where the data read should be placed in **a1**, and then executing a **SYSCALL** instruction. Once the process resumes, the number of characters actually transmitted is returned in **v0** if the read was successful. If the operation ends with a status other than "Character Received" (5), the negative of the device's status value is returned in **v0**.

Attempting to read from a terminal device to an address outside of the requesting U-proc's logical address space is an error and should result in the U-proc being terminated (SYS9).

The following C code can be used to request a SYS13:

```
int retValue = SYSCALL (READTERMINAL, char *virtAddr,
        0, 0);
```

Where the mnemonic constant `READTERMINAL` has the value of 13.

4.8   The Program Trap Exception Handler

For all Program Trap exceptions [Section 3.7.2], the nucleus either treats the exception as a SYS2 or "passes up" the handling of the exception if the offending process was provided a non-NULL value for its Support Structure pointer when it was created. [Section 3.7.2]

Assuming that the handling of the exception is to be passed up (non-NULL Support Structure pointer) and the appropriate `sup_exceptContext` fields of the Support Structure were correctly initialized, execution continues with the Support Level's general exception handler, which should then pass control to the Support Level's Program Trap exception handler. The processor state at the time of the exception will be in the Support Structure's corresponding `sup_exceptState` field. [Section 3.7]

The Support Level's Program Trap exception handler is to terminate the process in an orderly fashion; perform the same operations as a SYS9 request.[Section 4.7.1]

Important Point: If the process to be terminated is currently holding mutual exclusion on a Support Level semaphore (e.g. Swap Pool semaphore), mutual exclusion must first be released (SYS4) before invoking the Nucleus terminate command (SYS2).

4.9   Process Initialization and `test`

The final step in Nucleus initialization is the instantiation of a single process (kernel-mode on, interrupts enabled) whose **PC** is set to `test`. [Section 3.1] While `test` was the name/external reference to a function that exercised the Level 3/Phase 2 code, in Level 4/Phase 3 it will be used as the *instantiator process* (InstantiatorProcess).[3]

The InstantiatorProcess will perform the following tasks:

- Initialize the Level 4/Phase 3 data structures. These are:

    - The Swap Pool table and Swap Pool semaphore. [Section 4.4.1]

    - Each (potentially) sharable peripheral I/O device should have a semaphore defined for it. These semaphores will be used for mutual exclusion (protect access to each device's device registers) and therefore should all be initialized to one. Since terminal devices are actually two independent sub-devices, each terminal device should have two mutual exclusion semaphores defined for it: one for reading from the terminal and one for writing to the terminal. [Section 5.7-*pops*]

- Initialize and launch (SYS1) between 1 and 8 U-procs.

- Either:

    - Terminate (SYS2) after all of its U-proc "children" processes conclude. This will drive Process Count to zero, triggering the Nucleus to invoke **HALT**. [Section 3.2]

---

[3]One is, of course, free to rename this function, however, that will entail going back and editing one's already completed Level 3/Phase 2 code.

– Perform a P (SYS3) operation on a private semaphore initialized to 0. In this case, after all the U-proc "children" conclude, the Nucleus scheduler will detect deadlock and invoke **PANIC**. [Section 3.2]

Technical Point: A careful reading of the Level 4/Phase 3 specification reveals that there are actually no purposefully shared peripheral devices. Each of the [1..8] U-procs has its own flash device (backing store), printer, and terminal device(s). Hence, one does not actually *need* an array of mutual exclusion semaphores to protect access to device registers. However, for purposes of correctness (or more appropriate: to protect against erroneous behavior) and future phase compatibility, it is strongly recommended one define and use this array of mutual exclusion device register semaphores.

4.9.1 Initializing a U-proc

To launch a U-proc, one simply sets up the parameters for a SYS1, followed by the actual execution of the SYS1 Nucleus service. [Section 3.5.1]
The SYS1 Nucleus service takes two parameters:

- The initial processor state for the U-proc.

- A pointer to an initialized Support Structure for the U-proc.

Initial Processor State for a U-proc

Each U-proc's initial processor state should have its:

- **PC** (and s_t9) set to 0x8000.00B0; the address of the start of the **.text** section. [Section 10.3.1-*pops*]

- **SP** set to 0xC000.0000 [Section 4.2]

- **Status** set for user-mode with all interrupts and the processor Local Timer enabled.

- **EntryHi.ASID** set to the process's unique ID; an integer from [1..8]

Important Point: Each U-proc **MUST** be assigned a unique, non-zero **ASID**.

Initialization of a Support Structure for a U-proc

Since the Support Level will launch and execute between 1 and 8 U-procs, there needs to be a pool of (up to) 8 Support Structures.

The recommended approach is to declare a `static` array of 8 Support Structures in `test`. Using an index variable (**ASID**?) one can easily obtain the address of the next unused Support Structure to be initialized and used for the next U-proc launch (SYS1).

A Support Structure must contain all the fields necessary for the Support Level to support both paging and passed up **SYSCALL** services. [Section 3.7] This includes:

- `sup_asid`: The process's **ASID**.

- `sup_exceptState[2]`: The two processor state (`state_t`) areas where the processor state at the time of the exception is placed by the Nucleus for passing up exception handling to the Support Level.

- `sup_exceptContext[2]`: The two processor context (`context_t`) sets. Each context is a **PC/SP/Status** combination. These are the two processor contexts which the Nucleus uses for passing up exception handling to the Support Level.

- `sup_privatePgTbl[32]`: The process's Page Table.

- `sup_stackTLB[500]`: The stack area for the process's TLB exception handler. An integer array of 500 is a 2Kb area.

- `sup_stackGen[500]`: The stack area for the process's Support Level general exception handler.

Only the `sup_asid`, `sup_exceptContext[2]`, and `sup_privatePgTbl[32]` [Section 4.2.1] require initialization prior to issuing the SYS1.

To initialize a processor context area one performs the following:

- Set the two **PC** fields. One of them (0 - PGFAULTEXCEPT) should be set to the address of the Support Level's TLB handler, while the other one (1 - GENERALEXCEPT) should be set to the address of the Support Level's general exception handler.

- Set the two **Status** registers to: kernel-mode with all interrupts and the Processor Local Timer enabled.

- Set the two **SP** fields to utilize the two stack spaces allocated in the Support Structure. Stacks grow "down" so set the **SP** fields to the address of the end of these areas. e.g. `... = &(...sup_stackGen[499])`

4.10 Small Support Level Optimizations

There are a number of small optimizations that one can undertake to improve the performance/organization of the Support Level.

In no particular order:

- Update the TLB by using **TLBP** and **TLBWI** instead of **TLBCLR**. [Section 4.5.2]

- When a U-proc terminates, mark all of the frames it occupied as unoccupied. [Section 4.4.1].
  This has the potential to eliminate extraneous writes to the backing store.

- Improve the Pandos page replacement algorithm to first check for an unoccupied frame before selecting an occupied frame to use.
  This will turn an $O(1)$ operation into an $O(n)$ operation in exchange for fewer I/O (write) operations.

- Read each U-proc's header information and initialize the Page Table entries associated with each U-proc's **.text** pages as read only (**D** bit field set to 0/off). [Section 10.3.1-*pops*]

- Read Pandos's *.core* header information and situate the Swap Pool immediately after the **.text** and **.data** areas in RAM.
  This eliminates the need to overestimate the size of the operating system.

- Introduce a `masterSemaphore` for a more graceful conclusion/termination of `test`.
  `test` cannot conclude before all of its spawned U-procs, otherwise, the Nucleus will prematurely terminate them. Instead of blocking `test` on a semaphore and forcing a **PANIC** when all the spawned U-procs have concluded, one can implement a more graceful termination of `test`. [Section 4.9]

  Introduce a new Support Level-level semaphore; the zero-initialized *masterSemaphore*. After launching all the U-procs, `test` should repeatedly issue a SYS3 (V operation) on this semaphore. This loop should iterate UPROCMAX times: the number of U-proc's launched: [1..8]

Whenever a U-proc terminates, either normally, or abnormally, it should first perform a SYS4 (V operation) on the *masterSemaphore*. Hence, test will go to sleep n times, and be woken up n times, where n is the number of launched U-procs ($n \in [1..8]$). After this loop concludes, test concludes by issuing a SYS2, which should trigger a **HALT** by the Nucleus.

- Allocate per-U-proc TLB, and general exception handler stacks directly from RAM. [Section 4.9.1]
  Directly allocate the two stack spaces per U-proc (one for the Support Level's TLB exception handler, and one for the Support Level's general exception handler) from RAM, instead of as fields in the Support Structure. The recommended RAM space to be used are the frames directly below RAMTOP, avoid the actual last frame of RAM (stack page for test).

  Important Point: **SP** values are always the *end* of the area, not the start. Hence, to use the penultimate RAM frame as a U-proc's stack space for one of its Support Level handlers, one would assign the **SP** value to RAMTOP-PAGESIZE.

- Implement *allocate* and *deallocate* functionality for the Support Structures instead of directly accessing a static array. [Section 4.9.1]
  Instead of directly accessing elements of a static array of Support Structures, one can reuse the technique from Level 2/Phase 1 [Section 2.1]: Declare a null-initialized pointer to a Support Structure-free list (stack?) of unused Support Structures. Upon entry, test iterates over the static array of Support Structures, invoking a new deallocate method to add each Support Structure to the free list. Whenever a new Support Structure is needed to support a new U-proc, a call to allocate returns a pointer to a Support Structure, allocated from the free list. Furthermore, whenever a U-proc terminates (SYS9), a call is made to deallocate to return the Support Structure to the free list.

4.11 Nuts and Bolts

4.11.1 Initiating I/O Operations

A peripheral's *device driver* is typically made up of two parts: an *upper* part and a *lower* part.

The lower part is the code that handles the interrupt from the device upon completion of an operation. In Pandos this is handled by the Nucleus.

The upper part is the code that initiates an operation: the writing of some of the device's registers followed by a SYS5. In Pandos this code is distributed throughout the Support Level.

- For flash devices, the code to initiate reading and writing is part of (or at least called by) the Pager. [Section 4.4.2]

- For printer devices the code is localized in the SYS11 implementation code. [Section 4.7.3]

- For terminal devices the code is localized in the SYS12 & SYS13 implementation code. [Section 4.7.4]

Regardless of the device in question, to initiate an I/O operation, one must:

- Gain mutual exclusion over the device's device register. This is accomplished by executing a SYS3 operation on the appropriate Support Level semaphore.

- Write the device's **DATA0** field.

- Write the device's **COMMAND** field. Since a write into a **COMMAND** field immediately initiates an I/O operation, one must always supply the appropriate parameters in **DATA0** before writing the **COMMAND** field. [Chapter 5-*pops*]

- Issue a SYS5 with the appropriate parameters to block the I/O requesting process until the operation completes.

- Release mutual exclusion over the device's device register: Perform a SYS4 operation on the appropriate semaphore.

The Pandos Nucleus assumes that no device interrupt will occur *before* the initiating process has the opportunity to execute its SYS5. [Section 3.6.1]

To guarantee this, one must write the **COMMAND** field and execute the corresponding SYS5 instruction atomically. As with updating a Page Table and the TLB atomically [Section 4.5.3], this is done by disabling interrupts immediately prior to writing the **COMMAND** field, and reenabling interrupts immediately after the SYS5 instruction. Interrupts are disabled and enabled via the **STATUS** register (**setSTATUS**) [Section 7.1-*pops*]

4.11.2   Module Decomposition

One possible module decomposition is as follows:

1. initProc.c This module implements `test` and exports the Support Level's global variables. (e.g. device semaphores [Section 4.9], and optionally a `masterSemaphore` [Section 4.10]

2. vmSupport.c This module implements the TLB exception handler (The Pager). Since reading and writing to each U-proc's flash device is limited to supporting paging, this module should also contain the function(s) for reading and writing flash devices.

   Additionally, the Swap Pool table and Swap Pool semaphore are local to this module. Instead of declaring them globally in initProc.c they can be declared module-wide in vmSupport.c. The `test` function will now invoke a new "public" function `initSwapStructs` which will do the work of initializing both the Swap Pool table and accompanying semaphore.

   Technical Point: Since the code for the TLB-Refill event handler was replaced (without relocating the function), `uTLB_RefillHandler` should still be found in the Level 3/Phase 2 exceptions.c file.

3. sysSupport.c This module implements the Support Level's:

   - general exception handler. [Section 4.6]
   - **SYSCALL** exception handler. [Section 4.7]
   - Program Trap exception handler. [Section 4.8]

4.11.3   Accessing the `libumps` **Library**

Accessing the **CP0** registers and the BIOS-implemented services/instructions in C (e.g. **WAIT**, **LDST**) is via the `libumps` library. [Chapter 7-*pops*]
Simply include the line

```
#include ``/usr/include/umps3/umps/libumps.h''
```

in one's source files.[4]

4.12   Testing

There is a provided set of possible U-proc programs that will "exercise" your code. These programs will generate page faults in addition to issuing **SYSCALL**s 9-13 and purposefully causing Program Traps. [Appendix A]

The supplied U-proc programs also come with their own Makefile configured to compile, link (using the U-proc linker script, `crtsi.o`), create a corresponding flash device (a .umps file) [Section 11.2-*pops*], and preload the U-proc's load image on to a flash device.

The recommended directory structure is to create a testers directory parallel to the other Pandos directories: h, phase1, phase2, and phase3 [Section 1.2]

As with any non-trivial system, you are strongly encouraged to use the *make* program to maintain your code. A sample *Makefile* has been supplied. See Chapter 10 in the POPS reference for more compilation details.

Once your (nine?) source files (two from Phase 1, four from Phase 2, and three from Phase 3) have been correctly compiled, linked together (with appropriate linker script, `crtso.o`, and `libumps.o`), and post-processed with umps3-elf2umps (all performed by the sample *Makefile*), your code can be tested by launching the μMPS3 emulator. At a terminal prompt, enter:

umps3

One uses the μMPS3 Machine Configuration Panel [Section 12.2.1-*pops*] to set various parameters appropriate for testing Pandos:

- The TLB Floor Address must be set to either 0x4000.0000 or 0x8000.0000.

---

[4]The file libumps.h is part of the μMPS3 distribution.
/usr/include/umps3/umps/ is the recommended installation location for this file.

- The amount of "installed" RAM must be sufficiently large enough for the OS code, the Swap Pool and stack page for `test`. (e.g. 128 frames)

- Using the **Devices** tab one maps a flash device (.umps) "file" with the corresponding μMPS3 flash device. [Section 12.2.1-*pops*] Simply use the Browse button to locate the appropriate .umps file (in the testers directory) and *enable* the device via the checkbox.

Part II
Advanced Layers of Pandos

Phase 4 - Level 5: DMA Device Support

Level 4/Phase 3 provided support for character-based devices. [Section 4.7]
This phase provides support for block-based devices: disks and flash devices.

Pandos disk and flash devices are DMA devices in that they can directly read from/write to (physical) RAM. This differs from the character-based devices (terminals and printers) where the character to be written/read is placed into a device register. Therefore, each disk and flash device will have a Pandos DMA buffer (i.e. RAM frame) dedicated to it.

Disk devices are read/written on a sector by sector basis. Each μMPS3 disk sector is 4Kb in size.

Flash devices are read/written on a block by block basis. Each μMPS3 flash device block is 4Kb in size.

To perform a disk/flash read operation:

1. The requested disk sector/flash block is read into the device's DMA buffer.

2. The data is copied from the DMA buffer into the requesting U-proc's address space starting from the provided start address.

A write operation is isomorphic, only the two steps are reversed:

1. The data is copied from the requesting U-proc's address space into the device's DMA buffer.

2. The targeted disk sector/flash block is overwritten with the contents of the DMA buffer.

It is important to observe that the source (or sink) logical addresses are not required to be page aligned. Hence, the copying phase could trigger up to two distinct page faults.

5.1 DMA Buffers

μMPS3 can support up to eight disk devices and eight flash devices. Hence, sixteen 4Kb RAM frames need to be allocated to support these DMA devices.

The recommended location for these buffers are immediately above/after the swap pool. [Section 4.4.1]

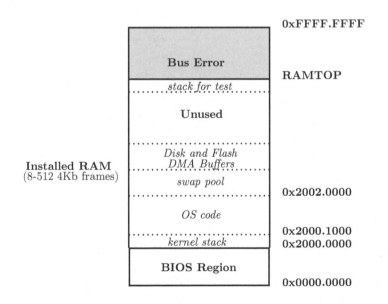

Figure 5.1: Memory Layout for the DMA Buffers

5.2   Disk Operations

From one perspective disk devices are three dimensional devices: cylinders (or tracks), surfaces (or heads) and sectors. From another perspective they are only one-dimensional: sectors. A disk device with x cylinders, y surfaces, and z sectors/track can be thought of being a (one dimensional) device with **sectorCnt** $= x * y * z$ sectors numbered $[0 \ldots (\textbf{sectorCnt} - 1)]$. The supported disk operations, since they only take a disk sector parameter (instead of a disk sector, surface#, and track#) assumes this one dimensional perspective for disk devices.

Attempting to write to (read from) a disk device from (into) an address outside of the requesting U-proc's logical address space is an error and should result in the U-proc being terminated (SYS9). Similarly, attempting to write to (read from) a disk sector outside of $[0 \ldots (\textbf{sectorCnt} - 1)]$ is an error and should result in the U-proc being terminated (SYS9).

Since disks can be created with differing dimensions [Section 11.1-*pops*], **sectorCnt** will differ from disk to disk. For a given disk, **sectorCnt** is equal to that disk's $maxcyl * maxhead * maxsect$ which are found in the device's **DATA1** device register field. [Section 5.3-*pops*]

While a disk read or write appears to U-procs as a singular operation, each read (or write) operation is actually two disk operations. A disk seek operation, and corresponding SYS5, followed by a disk read (or write) and its corresponding SYS5.

5.2.1   Disk_Put (SYS14)

This service provides *synchronous* I/O on a μMPS3 disk device. When requested, this service causes the requesting U-proc to be suspended until the disk write operation (both the seek and the write) has concluded. The SYS14 service is requested by the calling U-proc by placing the value 14 in **a0**, the logical address of the 4KB area to be written to the disk in **a1**, the disk number ([0...7]) in **a2**, the disk sector number to be written onto in **a3**, and then executing a **SYSCALL** instruction. Once the process resumes, **v0** is to contain the completion status of the disk operation. If the operation ends with a status other than "Device Ready" (1), the negative of the completion status is returned in **v0**.

The following C code can be used to request a SYS14:

```
int SYSCALL (DISK_PUT, int *logicalAddr, int diskNo,
        int sectNo);
```

Where the mnemonic constant `DISK_PUT` has the value of 14.

5.2.2 Disk_Get (SYS15)

This service provides *synchronous* I/O on a μMPS3 disk device. When requested, this service causes the requesting U-proc to be suspended until the disk read operation (both the seek and the read) has concluded.

The SYS15 service is requested by the calling U-proc by placing the value 15 in **a0**, the logical address of the 4KB area to contain the data from the disk in **a1**, the disk number ([0...7]) in **a2**, the disk sector number to be read from in **a3**, and then executing a **SYSCALL** instruction. Once the process resumes, **v0** is to contain the completion status of the disk operation. If the operation ends with a status other than "Device Ready" (1), the negative of the completion status is returned in **v0**.

The following C code can be used to request a SYS15:

```
int SYSCALL (DISK_GET, int *logicalAddr, int diskNo,
        int sectNo);
```

Where the mnemonic constant `DISK_GET` has the value of 15.

5.3 Flash Device Operations

μMPS3 flash devices are "random access" nonvolatile read/write devices which behave, essentially, as seek-free one-dimensional disk drives. Flash devices are read/written on a block by block basis. Each μMPS3 flash device block is 4Kb in size. [Section 5.4-*pops*]

Attempting to write to (read from) a flash device from (into) an address outside of the requesting U-proc's logical address space is an error and should result in the U-proc being terminated (SYS9). Similarly, attempting to write to (read from) a block outside of [0..(**MAXBLOCK**-1)] is an error and should result in the U-proc being terminated (SYS9).

Since flash devices can be created with differing dimensions [Section 11.2-*pops*], **MAXBLOCK** will differ from one flash device to another. For a given flash device, **MAXBLOCK** can be found in the device's **DATA1** device register field. [Section 5.4-*pops*]

5.3.1   Flash_Put (SYS16)

This services provides *synchronous* I/O on a μMPS3 flash device. When requested, this service causes the requesting U-proc to be suspended until the flash write operation has concluded.

The SYS16 service is requested by the calling U-proc by placing the value 16 in **a0**, the logical address of the 4KB area to be written to the flash device in **a1**, the flash device number ([0...7]) in **a2**, the block number to be written onto in **a3**, and then executing a **SYSCALL** instruction. Once the process resumes, **v0** is to contain the completion status of the flash operation. If the operation ends with a status other than "Device Ready" (1), the negative of the completion status is returned in **v0**.

The following C code can be used to request a SYS16:

```
int SYSCALL (FLASH_PUT, int *logicalAddr, int flashNo,
        int blockNo);
```

Where the mnemonic constant `FLASH_PUT` has the value of 16.

5.3.2   Flash_Get (SYS17)

This service provides *synchronous* I/O on a μMPS3 flash device. When requested, this service causes the requesting U-proc to be suspended until the flash read operation has concluded.

The SYS17 service is requested by the calling U-proc by placing the value 17 in **a0**, the logical address of the 4KB area to contain the data from the flash device in **a1**, the flash device number ([0...7]) in **a2**, the block number to be read from in **a3**, and then executing a **SYSCALL** instruction. Once the process resumes, **v0** is to contain the completion status of the flash operation. If the operation ends with a status other than "Device Ready" (1), the negative of the completion status is returned in **v0**.

The following C code can be used to request a SYS17:

```
int SYSCALL (FLASH_GET, int *logicalAddr, int flashNo,
        int blockNo);
```

Where the mnemonic constant `FLASH_GET` has the value of 17.

5.4 A Word About Backing Store

In Level 4/Phase 3, each U-proc was provided its own flash device preloaded with the U-proc's backing store data. [Section 4.2.2] One can continue to use this simplification even as one implements SYS16 and SYS17. The only caveat is that it should also be an error for a U-proc to access (read or write) any portion of a flash device being used as a backing store. Hence the potential reasons a SYS16 (or SYS17) request should fail (SYS9 - termination) is updated to:

1. An attempt to write to (read from) a flash device from (into) an address outside of the requesting U-proc's logical address space.

2. An attempt to write to (read from) a block outside of [32..(**MAXBLOCK-1**)]

Furthermore, there are two improvements one can elect to implement which remove the (unrealistic) simplification of providing each U-proc its own backing store device.

5.4.1 Dedicate a Disk as the Backing Store Device

Create an empty disk (e.g. DISK0) [Section 11.1-*pops*] to serve as the single backing store device for all U-procs.[1] Each U-proc will be assigned its own distinct 32 sectors for use as that U-proc's backing store. The mapping of **ASID** and **VPN** to DISK0 sector number is left to the Pandos author.

The InstantiatorProcess will now perform one additional step as part of U-proc initialization [Section 4.9]: Read the contents of the U-proc's assigned flash device/backing store information onto its assigned area on DISK0.

This operation can itself be done two different ways:

1. Simply copy the first 31 blocks from each flash device to DISK0; there is no need to copy of the initially empty stack page. This option copies a U-proc's complete (sans stack page) logical address space from the flash device to DISK0: Both the initialized portions and the empty/uninitialized portions.

---

[1]One must use the **Devices** tab on the μMPS3 Machine Configuration Panel to map the disk (.umps) "file" with the corresponding μMPS3 disk device. [Section 12.2.1-*pops*]

2. Copy the first block from each flash device to DISK0. Examine the U-proc's header information (situated at the beginning of this first block [Section 10.3.1-*pops*]) to learn how many more blocks to copy to DISK0. One need only copy the blocks containing the U-proc's **.text** and **.data**. The remainder of the U-proc's logical address space is uninitialized and need not be (unnecessarily) copied from the flash device to DISK0.

Since DISK0 is dedicated as the backing store device, U-procs must be prevented from performing reads/writes against this device. Hence, a SYS14 or SYS15 attempt to write to (read from) the backing store device (DISK0) is an error and should result in the U-proc being terminated (SYS9).

Technical Point: While having only a single backing store device is more realistic it does lead to performance degradation. The single device is now a bottleneck point for the Pager.

5.4.2   Supply ALL the U-procs from a Single Flash Device

In Level 4/Phase 3, each U-proc was provided its own flash device preloaded with the U-proc's backing store data. [Section 4.2.2] Instead of loading only one U-proc's logical image (backing store) on a flash device, provide one flash device containing all of the U-procs' logical images.

One limitation to this is the **umps3-mkdev** Device Creation Utility only allows the preloading of a single file on a flash device. [Section 11.2-*pops*]
To get around this limitation one needs to merge all of the U-procs' logical images one wishes to execute into one file.

The *.c source code files for a U-proc get compiled, linked, and post-processed to produce a *.aout.umps* file. It is this *.aout.umps* file that gets loaded onto a μMPS3 flash device when the device is created. [Section 10.6.2-*pops*]

One can, however, create a single Unix *tar* (Tape ARchive) file from many *.aout.umps* files. One then preloads this single tar file onto a flash device during its creation. [Section 11.2-*pops*]

The InstantiatorProcess now needs to read from a single flash device the information for U-proc initialization - the contents of each U-proc's logical image to be written to DISK0, the backing store device.

To accomplish this one needs to become familiar with the tar file format. While a complete description is beyond the scope of this text, it suffices to recognize that a tar file is an ordered collection of file objects (e.g. *.aout.umps*), each preceded by a 512 byte header. The header information contains, most important for this application, the file size rounded up to a multiple of 4Kb.[2]

While processing a single flash device preloaded with a tar file may appear intimidating; it is not. Each file appears, one after another with a header that indicates how many blocks long the *.aout.umps* file is.

One significant benefit from this is that InstantiatorProcess can now be configured to execute more than eight U-procs. While eight remains the concurrent multiprogramming limit (due only to the fixed number of terminal devices), one can reuse a given terminal device (**ASID**) after termination to read in a "next" U-proc from the input flash device for execution.

5.5 Nuts and Bolts

5.5.1 Initiating I/O Operations

A peripheral's *device driver* is typically made up of two parts: an *upper* part and a *lower* part.

The lower part is the code that handles the interrupt from the device upon completion of an operation. In Pandos this is handled by the Nucleus.

The upper part is the code that initiates an operation: the writing of some of the device's registers followed by a SYS5. Unlike the terminal (and printer) devices, these DMA devices (i.e. the device registers and corresponding DMA buffer) are shared devices. Hence, they must be accessed in a mutually exclusive manner.

Regardless of the device in question, to initiate a DMA I/O operation, one must:

- Gain mutual exclusion over the device's device register (and hence DMA buffer). This is accomplished by executing a SYS3 operation on the appropriate Support Level semaphore. [Section 4.9]

- Write the starting address of the appropriate DMA buffer in the device's **DATA0** field.

- Write the device's **COMMAND** field. Since a write into a **COMMAND** field immediately initiates an I/O operation, one must always supply the

---

[2]Unix tar files use a 512 byte blocking factor by default. However, this can be changed to 4Kb via a command line argument.

appropriate parameters in **DATA0** before writing the **COMMAND** field. [Chapter 5-*pops*]

- Issue a SYS5 with the appropriate parameters to block the I/O requesting U-proc until the operation completes.

- Release mutual exclusion over the device's device register: perform a SYS4 operation on the appropriate semaphore.

The Pandos Nucleus assumes that no device interrupt will occur *before* the initiating process has the opportunity to execute its SYS5. [Section 3.6.1]
To guarantee this, one must write the **COMMAND** field and execute the corresponding SYS5 instruction atomically. This is done by disabling interrupts immediately prior to writing the **COMMAND** field, and reenabling interrupts immediately after the SYS5 instruction. Interrupts are disabled and enabled via the **STATUS** register (**setSTATUS**) [Section 7.1-*pops*]

5.5.2 Module Decomposition

One possible module decomposition is to develop a separate module which implements these four new **SYSCALL**s. (e.g. deviceSupportDMA.c)
The functionality of both SYS16 & SYS17 already exists in the Level 4/Phase 3 Pager. [Section 4.11.2] One should migrate this code out of vmSupport.c and into deviceSupportDMA.c to facilitate code sharing. (e.g. Have the Pager, SYS16, and SYS17 all make use of the single function flashOperation located in deviceSupportDMA.c)
Similarly, one could migrate the code supporting character-based devices (SYS11 – SYS13) into a new file; devSupportChar.c or merge ALL device support functionality into a single file; deviceSupport.c

5.6   Testing

One of the provided U-proc test programs (diskIOtest.c) will "exercise" your SYS14/SYS15 code. [Appendix A]

Never under any circumstances take a sleeping pill and a laxative on the same night.

Dave Barry

Phase 5 - Level 6: The Delay Facility

Level 6/Phase 5 implements one new **SYSCALL** which causes the requesting U-proc to be temporarily "put to sleep" (i.e. delayed) for a specified number of seconds, n. This phase is representative of a daemon process.

The requesting U-proc is to be delayed at least n seconds and not substantially longer. Since the Nucleus controls low-level scheduling decisions, all this phase can ensure is that the requesting U-proc not be "schedulable" until n seconds have elapsed and that it becomes schedulable shortly thereafter.

6.1 Delay (SYS18)

This service causes the executing U-proc to be delayed for n seconds.

The Delay or SYS18 service is requested by the calling U-proc by placing the value 18 in **a0**, the number of seconds to be delayed in **a1**, and then executing a **SYSCALL** instruction.

Attempting to request a Delay for less than 0 seconds is an error and should result in the U-proc begin terminated (SYS9).

The following C code can be used to request a SYS18:

```
void SYSCALL (DELAY, int secCnt, 0, 0);
```

Where the mnemonic constant `DELAY` has the value of 18.

6.2   Delay Facility

The SYS18 Delay facility allows a requesting U-proc to be temporarily "put to sleep" for a specified number of seconds. A process that is neither the current process nor sitting on the Ready Queue can be considered to be "sleeping" (i.e. blocked). There are two issues that need addressing: where to place the U-proc while it is sleeping, and how to keep track of which U-proc's are sleeping so they can be awoken (i.e. placed on the Ready Queue) at the appropriate time.

6.2.1   Where to Store Sleeping U-proc's

Access to the nucleus is limited solely to requesting SYS1-SYS8 services. Therefore the only way to put a U-proc to sleep (i.e. keep it off of the Ready Queue) is to block the U-proc on a semaphore. The Support Structure should therefore contain a semaphore; the U-proc's private semaphore. Since this is a *synchronization* semaphore, it should be initialized to zero. Hence a SYS3/P operation on this semaphore will cause the U-proc to block.

A SYS18 is therefore a request to perform a P (SYS3) operation on the U-proc's private semaphore.

6.2.2   Keeping Track of Sleeping U-proc's

The Delay Facility needs to maintain a list of sleeping U-proc's. The following implementation is suggested: Maintain a sorted, NULL-terminated, single, linearly linked list (using the `d_next` field) of delay_event descriptor nodes (`delayd_t`) whose head is pointed to by the variable `delayd_h`. The list `delayd_h` points to will represent the list of pending "wake up calls:" the *Active Delay* List (ADL). Keep the ADL sorted in ascending order using the `d_wakeTime` field as the sort key.

Maintain a second list of delay_event descriptor nodes, the *delaydFree* list, to hold the unused delay_event descriptor nodes. This list, whose head is pointed to by the variable `delaydFree_h`, is kept, like the semdFree lists, as a NULL-terminated, single, linearly linked list (using the `d_next` field). [Section 2.4]

The delay_event descriptor nodes themselves should be declared, like the ASL's semaphore descriptors, as a `static` array of size UPROCMAX of type `delayd_t`. The fields of a delay_event descriptor node (`delayd_t`) are:

- A `delayd_t *d_next` pointer field.

- A `int d_wakeTime` field. This field should record the time of day (microseconds since the system was last booted/reset) the U-proc should be woken, and NOT n, the requested number of sleep seconds.

- A `support_t *d_supStruct` pointer to a Support Structure, denoting the sleeping U-proc's identity.

When a U-proc requests some "quiet time," in addition to performing a P (SYS3) operation on the U-proc's private semaphore, a delay_event descriptor node needs to be allocated from the delaydFree list, populated with appropriate values, and inserted into the ADL.

Periodically, the ADL needs to be examined to determine if a U-proc's wake time has passed. To accomplish this the Support Level will launch a special Support Level process (i.e. a daemon): the Delay Daemon. The Delay Daemon will repeat forever:

1. Request a Wait_For_Clock (SYS7) nucleus service.

2. Upon resumption of execution, examine the ADL, removing all delay_event descriptor nodes whose wake time has passed. For each delay_event descriptor node whose wake time has passed, perform a V (SYS4) operation on the U-proc's private semaphore and return the delay_event descriptor node to the delaydFree list.

Hence, the Delay Daemon will wake every 100 milliseconds (i.e. a pseudo-clock tick event), examine the ADL, waking up U-proc's if their delay has expired, and then return to sleep (SYS7). The Delay Daemon will run in kernel-mode using the kernel **ASID** value (zero) with all interrupts enabled.

There is no reason to make the ADL doubly linked, though for greater ADL traversal efficiency one may opt to place a dummy node at either the tail or both the head and tail of the ADL. In this case the size of the static array will increase by either one or two.

6.3   Nuts and Bolts

On the surface, there is a lot in common between the Delay Facility and the ASL. Both modules initialize a free list of unallocated nodes and have a singly linked, sorted, NULL-terminated "active" list. Furthermore, both modules have two list pointers (active and free) in addition to an initialization function which statically declares an array of descriptor nodes and places all these nodes on the free list. As with the ASL, the ADL's active list, for list traversal efficiency, should also contain at least one dummy node (tail).

6.3.1   Implementing SYS18

The SYS18 service performs two functions:

1. Allocate a delay_event descriptor node from the free list, populate it, and insert it into its proper location on the active list.

2. Perform a P (SYS3) operation on the U-proc's private semaphore; a field in the Support Structure.

Two considerations must be taken into account:

- The ADL is a shared data structure, accessed by both U-procs via SYS18 and the Delay Daemon. Hence, access to the ADL must be done in a mutually exclusive manner to avoid race conditions. Therefore, the ADL must also implement a mutual exclusion semaphore (i.e. initialized to one). This semaphore must be SYS3/P'ed prior to any access of the ADL, and then SYS4/V'ed upon conclusion of any access.

- At the conclusion of SYS18 is a call to SYS3/P on the U-proc's private semaphore. However, this call must be made *after* the SYS4/V call on the ADL semaphore; otherwise the U-proc will be put to sleep while holding mutual exclusion over the ADL. Hence, one must first release the mutual exclusion over the ADL semaphore (SYS4/V) and then block the calling U-proc on its private semaphore (SYS3/P). Furthermore, these two actions must be done atomically.

The complete sequence of steps to be performed for a SYS18 is:

1. Check the seconds parameter and terminate (SYS9) the U-proc if the wait time is negative.

2. Obtain mutual exclusion over the ADL: SYS3/P on the ADL semaphore.

3. Allocate a delay_event descriptor node from the free list, populate it and insert it into its proper location on the active list. If this operation is unsuccessful, terminate (SYS9) the U-proc – after releasing mutual exclusion over the ADL.

4. Release mutual exclusion over the ADL: SYS4/V on the ADL semaphore AND execute a SYS3/P on the U-proc's private semaphore atomically. This will block the executing U-proc.

5. Return control (**LDST**) to the U-proc at the instruction immediately following the SYS18. This step will not be executed until after the U-proc is awoken.

6.3.2   Implementing the Delay Daemon

The code for the Delay Daemon is a simple infinite loop:

1. Execute a SYS7: wait for the next 100 millisecond time span (i.e. pseudo clock tick) to pass.

2. Obtain mutual exclusion over the ADL: SYS3/P on the ADL semaphore.

3. "Process" the ADL active list and for each delay_event descriptor node whose wake up time has passed:

   (a) Perform a SYS4/V on that U-proc's private semaphore.

   (b) Deallocate the delay_event descriptor node and return it to the free list.

4. Release mutual exclusion over the ADL: SYS4/V on the ADL semaphore.

6.3.3   Initializing the ADL

Initializing the ADL is facilitated by the InstantiatorProcess [Section 4.9] which invokes the ADL function `initADL()`.
Initializing the ADL is a two-step process:

1. Add each element from the static array of delay_event descriptor nodes to the free list and initialize the active list (zero, one or two dummy nodes).

2. Initialize and launch (SYS1) the Delay Daemon.

The Delay Daemon is a process where

- The **PC** (and s_t9) is set to the function implementing the Delay Daemon. [Section 6.3.2]

- The **SP** is set to an unused frame at the end of RAM. The last frame of RAM is already allocated as the stack page for test. Whether the penultimate frame of RAM is available is dependent on the Level 4/Phase 3 approach for allocating the two stack spaces per U-proc: one for the Support Level's TLB exception handler, and one for the Support Level's general exception handler. If these stack spaces are allocated as part of the Support Structure, then the penultimate RAM frame is to be used, otherwise allocate a frame above/below the stack frames allocated for the U-proc exception handlers. [Section 4.10]

- The **Status** register is set to kernel-mode with all interrupts enabled.

- The **EntryHi.ASID** is set to the kernel **ASID**: zero.

Finally, the Support Structure SYS1 parameter should be NULL.

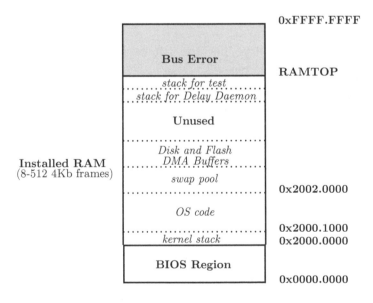

Figure 6.1: Memory Layout for the Delay Daemon Stack

6.3.4 Breaking Down the Delay Facility Module

The Delay Facility should be encapsulated in a single file: e.g. delayDaemon.c. This file should contain:

- initADL: The function to initialize the ADL. [Section 6.3.3]

- The function to implement SYS18. [Section 6.3.1]

- The function containing the code for the Delay Daemon. [Section 6.3.2]

- Functions for maintaining the ADL's freelist and active list: allocate, deallocate, node insertion, and node removal.

6.4 Testing

One of the provided U-proc test programs (delayTest.c) will "exercise" your SYS18 Delay Daemon code. [Appendix A]

Man is a slow, sloppy and brilliant thinker; the machine is fast, accurate and stupid.

William M. Kelly

7

Phase 6 - Level 7: Cooperating User Processes

There are two primary paradigms for processes to cooperate: message passing or shared memory. Pandos takes the shared memory approach.[1]

In addition to providing a shared logical address space, there must also be a means of safely adjudicating its use so as to avoid race conditions. Level 7/Phase 6 implements two new **SYSCALL**s which allow for requesting U-procs to perform P and V semaphore operations on shared logical addresses.

7.1 A Shared Logical Address Space

While the first half of **kuseg** is reserved for each U-proc's private logical address space (0x8000.0000... 0xC000.0000), the second/upper half (0xC000.0000... 0xFFFF.FFFF) is reserved as a logical address space (**kuseg**$_{share}$) shared among all executing U-procs.

In keeping with Pandos's "representative" approach, only the first n frames of

---

[1]Message passing can also be implemented, but one must first provide Networking Support. [Chapter 1]

kuseg$_{share}$ will be available, where n can be any value from [1..32] - implementor's choice.

Figure 7.1: **kuseg** Logical Address Layout

There are a number of address translation-based bookkeeping tasks that must be completed to implement **kuseg**$_{share}$.

7.1.1 A Shared Page Table

In addition to each U-proc's private Page Table there now needs to one additional *global* Page Table for the n pages of **kuseg**$_{share}$. Each entry should be initialized as follows:

- The **VPN** field will be set to [0xC0000..0xC000n] for the n entries.

- The **ASID** field should be set to zero.

- The **D** bit field will be set to 1 (on) - each page is write-cnablcd.

- The **V** bit field will be set to 0 (off) - the entry is NOT valid. i.e. A copy of this page is not also currently residing in RAM.

- The **G** bit field will be set to 1 (on) - each page is globally accessible regardless of the accessor's **ASID**. [Section 6.3.2-*pops*]

7.1.2   Updates to the TLB-Refill event Handler

The TLB-Refill event Handler (`uTLB_RefillHandler`) now needs to update the TLB from one of two different Page Tables, depending on the **VPN** of the missing TLB entry.

- **VPN** values less than 0xC0000 are handled in the usual manner, using a Page Table entry from the Current Process's Page Table. [Section 4.2.2]

- **VPN** values greater than or equal to 0xC0000 are handled using a Page Table entry from the **kuseg**$_{share}$'s global Page Table.

7.1.3   Backing Store for the Shared Logical Address Space

As with all logical address spaces, the n **kuseg**$_{share}$ pages need a backing store location. However, given the nature of the **kuseg**$_{share}$, the backing store area does not need to be initialized.

The backing store location of the n **kuseg**$_{share}$ pages is dependent on how the backing store for the U-procs is handled. [Section 5.4]

- If DISK0 is used, one simply needs to assign n unused sectors as the backing store for the n **kuseg**$_{share}$ pages.

- If each U-proc is using its preloaded flash device for its backing store [Section 4.2.2], the recommendation is to use blocks [32..(32+n-1)] on FLASH0 as the backing store for the n **kuseg**$_{share}$ pages. This has the concomitant effect of increasing the number of blocks which are "off limits," for FLASH0, with respect to Flash_Put (SYS16) & Flash_Get (SYS17) operations.

7.1.4   Updates to the Pager

The Pager also needs to be updated in a manner similar to the TLB-Refill event Handler. Any update to a Page Table must first check the **VPN** to determine which Page Table is to be updated: a U-proc's private Page Table or the shared **kuseg**$_{share}$ Page Table. Similarly, the **VPN** will determine which backing store area is to written to/read from.

There is one unique wrinkle that the Pager must now account for. Consider the case where the Pager is handling a page fault on a shared page and another U-proc generates a page fault for the same page. Because of mutual exclusion, this second U-proc will wait (on the Swap Pool semaphore) until the conclusion of the first U-proc's page fault. When the second U-proc eventually continues, it will proceed in the Pager as if the shared page is still missing – when in fact it was just read in as a result of the first U-proc's page fault.

To handle this case the Pager must be amended in the following manner. Perform the same initial five steps as before. [Section 4.4.2] After gaining mutual exclusion over the Swap Pool table (SYS3 – P operation on the Swap Pool semaphore):

1. If the **VPN** for the missing page belongs in **kuseg**$_{share}$, check the **kuseg**$_{share}$ Page Table to see if the page is still missing.

2. If yes, continue with normal page fault processing. If no, skip to the end of the Pager: Return control to the Current Process to retry the instruction that caused the page fault: **LDST** on the saved exception state.

7.2 A Semaphore Service for Logical Addresses

The Semaphore Service for logical addresses allows a requesting U-proc to request a P or V operation on a semaphore with a logical address in **kuseg**$_{share}$. Since U-proc's run in user-mode and are restricted to only using logical addresses, the Nucleus SYS3/SYS4 service is not available to U-proc's wishing to coordinate their cooperation (i.e. shared use of **kuseg**$_{share}$) through the use of semaphores.

7.2.1 P_Logical_Semaphore (SYS19)

This service performs a P operation on a semaphore whose address is logical (in **kuseg**$_{share}$).

The P or SYS19 service is requested by the calling U-proc by placing the value 19 in **a0**, the *logical* address of the semaphore to be P'ed in **a1**, and then executing a **SYSCALL** instruction.

Attempting to perform a P operation on an address outside of **kuseg**$_{share}$ is an error and should result in the U-proc being terminated (SYS9).

The following C code can be used to request a SYS19:

```
void SYSCALL (PSEMLOGICAL, int *semAddr, 0, 0)
```

Where the mnemonic constant PSEMLOGICAL has the value of 19.

7.2.2   V_Logical_Semaphore (SYS20)

This service performs a V operation on a semaphore whose address is logical (in **kuseg**$_{share}$).

The V or SYS20 service is requested by the calling U-proc by placing the value 20 in **a0**, the *logical* address of the semaphore to be V'ed in **a1**, and then executing a **SYSCALL** instruction.

Attempting to perform a V operation on an address outside of **kuseg**$_{share}$ is an error and should result in the U-proc being terminated (SYS9).

The following C code can be used to request a SYS20:

```
void SYSCALL (VSEMLOGICAL, int *semAddr, 0, 0)
```

Where the mnemonic constant VSEMLOGICAL has the value of 20.

7.3   Implementation Details

As with the Delay Facility [Chapter 6], there are two issues that need addressing for the implementation of this Logical Semaphore Service: where to place a U-proc blocked on a logical-address semaphore, and how to keep track of which U-proc's are blocked on a given semaphore so that they can be awoken (i.e. placed on the Ready Queue) at the appropriate time; when a V (SYS20) operation is requested for the specified semaphore.

The solution described below is very similar to the Delay Facility. [Section 6.2] The primary difference is that instead of a Delay Daemon, U-procs become unblocked/woken by another U-proc executing a V operation (SYS20).

7.3.1   Where to Store Blocked U-proc's

When a U-proc performs a P (SYS19) operation on a logical-address semaphore and the value of the semaphore becomes < 0 (i.e. the U-proc is to be blocked), the Logical Semaphore Service should perform a P (SYS3) operation on the requesting U-proc's private semaphore. [Section 6.2.1]

7.3.2 Keeping Track of Blocked U-proc's

The Logical Semaphore Service needs to maintain a list of U-proc's blocked because of a P (SYS19) operation. The following implementation is suggested: Maintain a queue of logical_semaphore descriptor nodes (`logicalSemd_t`). This queue, as with *pcb* queues [Section 2.2], should be double, circularly linked, and pointed to by a tail pointer (`blockedUprocs`). The queue `blockedUprocs` points to will represent the (partially) ordered collection of U-proc's blocked because of a P (SYS19) operation: the *Active Logical Semaphore* List (ALSL).

Maintain a second list of logical_semaphore descriptor nodes, the *logicalSemd-Free* list, to hold the unused logical_semaphore descriptor nodes. This list, whose head is pointed to by the variable `logicalSemdFree_h`, is kept, like the delaydFree, pcbFree, and semdFree lists, as a NULL-terminated single linearly linked list (using the `ls_next` field).

The logical_semaphore descriptor nodes themselves should be declared, like the ASL's semaphore descriptors, as a `static` array of size UPROCMAX of type `logicalSemd_t`.

The fields of a logical_semaphore descriptor node (`logicalSemd_t`) are:

- A `logicalSemd_t *ls_next` pointer field.

- A `logicalSemd_t *ls_prev` pointer field.

- A `int ls_semAddr` field. The logical address of the semaphore.

- A `support_t *ls_supStruct` pointer to a Support Structure, denoting the blocked U-proc's identity.

When a U-proc is to be blocked as a result of a P (SYS19) request, in addition to performing a P (SYS3) operation on the U-proc's private semaphore, a logical_semaphore descriptor node needs to be allocated from the logicalSemdFree list, populated with appropriate values, and enqueued onto the ALSL.

When a U-proc is to be unblocked as a result of a V (SYS20) request, a linear search, starting from the head of the queue, is made of the ALSL for a logical_semaphore descriptor node with a matching `ls_semAddr` field. This node is removed from the ALSL and returned to the logicalSemdFree list. Finally a V (SYS4) operation is performed on the indicated U-proc's private semaphore.

By enqueueing new nodes at the end/tail of ALSL, and searching for matching semaphore addresses linearly starting from the ALSL's head, proper semantics are maintained when there is more than one U-proc blocked on the same semaphore.

7.4   Nuts and Bolts

On the surface, there is a lot in common between the Logical Semaphore Service and both the Delay facility and the ASL. Each module initializes a free list of unallocated nodes in addition to an "active" list. Furthermore, each module has two list pointers (active and free) in addition to an initialization function which statically declares an array of descriptor nodes and places all these nodes on the free list.

7.4.1   Implementing SYS19

The SYS19 service performs the following function:
Decrement the semaphore and if < 0 block the executing U-proc by doing the following, otherwise, return control (**LDST**) to the U-proc at the instruction immediately following the SYS19.

1. Allocate a logical_semaphore descriptor node from the free list, populate it, and insert it into its proper location on the active list (ALSL).

2. Perform a P (SYS3) operation on the U-proc's private semaphore; a field in the Support Structure.

Two considerations must be taken into account:

- The ALSL is a shared data structure, accessed by both the SYS19 code and the SYS20 code. Hence, access to the ALSL must be done in a mutually exclusive manner to avoid race conditions. Therefore, the Logical Semaphore Service must also implement a mutual exclusion ALSL semaphore (i.e. initialized to one). This semaphore must be SYS3/P'ed prior to any access of the ALSL, and then SYS4/V'ed upon conclusion of any access.

- At the conclusion of SYS19 is a call to SYS3/P on the U-proc's private semaphore. However, this call must be made *after* the SYS4/V call on the ALSL semaphore; otherwise the U-proc will be put to sleep while holding mutual exclusion over the ALSL. Hence, one must first release the mutual exclusion over the ALSL semaphore (SYS4/V) and then block the calling U-proc on its private semaphore (SYS3/P). Furthermore, these two actions must be done atomically.

The complete sequence of steps to be performed for a SYS19 is:

1. Check the `semAddr` parameter and terminate (SYS9) the U-proc if the address is not in the first n pages of **kuseg**$_{share}$.

2. Decrement the semaphore and if its value is < 0, continue with the following steps, otherwise return control (**LDST**) to the U-proc at the instruction immediately following the SYS19.

3. Obtain mutual exclusion over the ALSL: SYS3/P on the ALSL semaphore.

4. Allocate a logical_semaphore descriptor node from the free list, populate it and enqueue it at the tail of the ALSL. If this operation is unsuccessful, terminate (SYS9) the U-proc – after releasing mutual exclusion over the ALSL.

5. Release mutual exclusion over the ALSL: SYS4/V on the ALSL semaphore AND execute a SYS3/P on the U-proc's private semaphore atomically. This will block the executing U-proc.

6. Return control (**LDST**) to the U-proc at the instruction immediately following the SYS19. This step will not be executed until after the U-proc is awoken.

7.4.2 Implementing SYS20

The SYS20 service performs the following function:
Increment the semaphore and if ≤ 0 unblock the U-proc that has been blocked the longest on this semaphore by doing the following, and then return control (**LDST**) to the U-proc at the instruction immediately following the SYS20.

1. Find and deallocate the "oldest" logical_semaphore descriptor node matching the given `semAddr` from the ALSL.

2. Perform a V (SYS4) operation on the private semaphore of the U-proc represented by the newly deallocated logical_semaphore descriptor node.

Since the ALSL is a shared data structure, access to it must be done in a mutually exclusive manner. Hence, the ALSL semaphore must be SYS3/P'ed prior to any access of the ALSL, and then SYS4/V'ed upon conclusion of any access.

The complete sequence of steps to be performed for a SYS20 is:

1. Check the `semAddr` parameter and terminate (SYS9) the U-proc if the address is not in the first n pages of **kuseg**$_{share}$.

2. Increment the semaphore and if its value is ≤ 0, continue with the following steps, otherwise return control (**LDST**) to the U-proc at the instruction immediately following the SYS19.

3. Obtain mutual exclusion over the ALSL: SYS3/P on the ALSL semaphore.

4. Linearly search the ALSL, starting from the queue's head, for a logical_semaphore descriptor node whose `ls_semAddr` matches the `semAddr` SYS20 parameter.

5. If no matching node is found, release mutual exclusion over the ALSL (SYS4 on the ALSL semaphore) and return control (**LDST**) to the U-proc at the instruction immediately following the SYS19, otherwise continue.

6. Deallocate the matching node from the ALSL and perform a V (SYS4) operation on the private semaphore of the U-proc represented by the newly deallocated logical_semaphore descriptor node.

7. Release mutual exclusion over the ALSL: SYS4/V on the ALSL semaphore.

8. Return control (**LDST**) to the U-proc at the instruction immediately following the SYS19.

7.4.3 Initializing the ALSL

Initializing the ALSL is facilitated by the InstantiatorProcess [Section 4.9] which invokes the ALSL function `initALSL()`.
To initialize the ALSL:

1. Add each element from the static array of logical_semaphore descriptor nodes to the free list (logicalSemdFree).

2. set the active list pointer (`blockedUprocs`) to NULL.

7.4.4 Breaking Down the Logical Semaphore Service

The Delay Facility should be encapsulated in a single file: e.g. alsl.c. This file should contain:

- initALSL: The function to initialize the ALSL. [Section 7.4.3]

- The function to implement SYS19. [Section 7.4.1]

- The function to implement SYS20. [Section 7.4.2]

- Functions for maintaining the ALSL's freelist and active list: allocate, deallocate, node search, node insertion, and node removal.

7.5 Testing

Two of the provided U-proc test programs (pvTestA.c & pvTestB.c) will "exercise" your SYS19 & SYS20 P/V for logical addresses code. [Appendix A]

Provided Test Files

A.1 Level 2/Phase 1 Test

One test file is provided for Level 2/Phase 1: p1test.c
This test program reports on its progress by writing messages to TERMINAL0. These messages are also added to one of two memory buffers; errbuf for error messages and okbuf for all other messages. At the conclusion of the test program, either successful or unsuccessful, μMPS3 will display a final message and then enter an infinite loop. The final message will either be System Halted for successful termination, or Kernel Panic for unsuccessful termination.

A.2 Level 3/Phase 2 Test

Another test file is provided for Level 3/Phase 2: p2test.c
This test code assumes that the TLB Floor Address has been set to any value except VM OFF. The value of the TLB Floor Address is a user configurable value set via the μMPS3 Machine Configuration Panel. [Chapter 12]

The test program reports on its progress by writing messages to TERMINAL0. At the conclusion of the test program, either successful or unsuccessful, μMPS3 will display a final message and then enter an infinite loop. The final message

94

will either be **System Halted** for successful termination, or **Kernel Panic** for unsuccessful termination.

A.3 Level 4/Phase 3 Test Files

Test files for Level 4/Phase 3 consist of U-procs. The supplied U-proc programs also come with their own **Makefile** configured to compile, link (using the U-proc linker script, `crtsi.o`), create a corresponding flash device (a .**umps** file) [Section 11.2-*pops*], and preload the U-proc's load image on to a flash device. See Chapter 10 in the POPS reference for more compilation details.

The recommended directory structure is to create a **testers** directory parallel to the other Pandos directories: **h**, **phase1**, **phase2**, **phase3**, etc. [Section 1.2]

To run multiple U-procs in their identically configured logical address space (**kuseg**), the TLB Floor Address must be set to either 0x4000.0000 or 0x8000.0000. The value of the TLB Floor Address is a user configurable value set via the μMPS3 Machine Configuration Panel. [Chapter 12-*pops*]

One also uses the μMPS3 Machine Configuration Panel to map a flash device's .**umps** "file" with the corresponding μMPS3 flash device. [Section 12.2.1-*pops*] Simply use the **Browse** button to locate the appropriate .**umps** file (in the **testers** directory) and *enable* the device via the checkbox.

The supplied test files for Level 4/Phase 3 are:

1. **fibTen.c** - This *long* compute job recursively computes the tenth fibonacci number. This program calls Terminate (SYS9) and Write_To_Terminal (SYS12). It is a simple matter to create isomorphic versions (e.g. **fibNine**) for controlled concurrency testing, as well as to direct output to a printer (Write_To_Printer - SYS11) instead of the terminal. Finally, instead of hardcoding 10, an interactive version is easily created using Read_From_Terminal (SYS13) to acquire, from a user, which fibonacci number should be computed.

2. **printerTest.c** - A trivial program which calls Terminate (SYS9), Write_To_Printer (SYS11), and Write_To_Terminal (SYS12).

3. **strConcat.c** - Exercises Terminate (SYS9), Write_To_Terminal (SYS12) and Read_From_Terminal (SYS13). Two different strings are read in from the user and their concatenated version is then written back to the terminal. **terminalReader.c** is a simpler "echo" program.

4. terminalTest.c - A trivial program which calls Terminate (SYS9) and Write_To_Terminal (SYS12). It is a simple matter to create isomorphic versions (e.g. terminal-Test1.c for controlled concurrency testing.

5. timeOfDay.c - Exercises Get_TOD (SYS10), and Write_To_Terminal (SYS12). At its conclusion it attempts to (illegally) execute a SYS6 which should cause the program to terminate.

6. swapStress.c - Exercises Terminate (SYS9) and Write_To_Terminal (SYS12). However, it also writes values into ten additional pages of the U-proc's logical address space forcing the Pager to perform page replacements. Finally, termination should be caused by providing an illegal address to a SYS12 operation. SYS9 is only invoked if Pandos failed to terminate the program due to the resulting error.

Each of these programs uses (i.e. # includes) a common set of constants (tconst.h) and a print to device (printer or terminal) function (print.c & print.h).

A.4   Additional Test Files

The following additional test files are provided for exercising the **SYSCALL**s from the additional layers of Pandos.

1. disklOtest.c - Exercises Disk_Put (SYS14) and Disk_Get (SYS15) by writing special values into various disk sectors and then reading them back to check the correctness of the operation. Finally, termination is caused by various illegal operations; which if none successfully cause termination, a final call to SYS9 is made.

2. delayTest.c - Exercises Delay (SYS18) in a manner very similar to time-OfDay.c

3. pvTestA.c & pvTestB.c - Exercises P_Logical_Semaphore (SYS19) and V_Logical_Semaphore (SYS20). Using the first page of $\mathbf{kuseg}_{share}$, these two processes operate in a producer/consumer mode using semaphores (also from the first page of $\mathbf{kuseg}_{share}$) for coordination.

A.4.1 New Test Files

One need not be limited by the small set of provided test files. Pandos authors are strongly encouraged to write their own programs to run on Pandos. There are very few experiences in computing more satisfying then running one's own program on one's own operating system!

Bibliography

[1] ALVISI, L., AND SCHNEIDER, F. A graphical interface for CHIP. Tech. rep., Cornell University, 1996. Technical Report TR 96-1587.

[2] BABAOGLU, O., BUSSAN, M., DRUMMOND, R., AND SCHNEIDER, F. Documentation for the CHIP computer system, 1988.

[3] BABAOGLU, O., AND SCHNEIDER, F. The HOCA operating system specifications, 1990.

[4] DIJKSTRA, E. The structure of the THE-multiprogramming system. *Commun. ACM 11*, 3 (may 1968).

[5] GOLDWEBER, M., AND DAVOLI, R. *μMPS Principles of Operation*. Lulu.com, 2005.

[6] GOLDWEBER, M., AND DAVOLI, R. *Student Guide to the Kaya Operating System Project*. Lulu.com, 2005.

[7] GOLDWEBER, M., AND DAVOLI, R. *μMPS2 Principles of Operation*. Lulu.com, 2011.

[8] GOLDWEBER, M., AND DAVOLI, R. *Student Guide to the Kaya Operating System Project*, 2 ed. Lulu.com, 2011.

[9] GOLDWEBER, M., AND DAVOLI, R. *μMPS3 Principles of Operation*. Lulu.com, 2020.

[10] MORSIANI, M. ICARO.S resource page. http://www.cs.unibo.it/mps/icaros.html.

[11] MORSIANI, M. MPS resource page. http://www.cs.unibo.it/mps.

[12] MORSIANI, M., AND DAVOLI, R. Learning operating systems structure and implementation through the MPS computer system simulator. In *Proceedings of the 30th SIGCSE Technical Symposium on Computer Science Education* (1999).